IN THE NAME OF MARX

IN THE NAME OF MARX

Murzban Jal

AAKAR

In the Name of Marx
Murzban Jal

First Published 2018
Reprinted 2024

ISBN 978-93-5002-539-0

Published by
AAKAR BOOKS
28 E Pocket IV, Mayur Vihar Phase I,
Delhi 110 091 India
aakarbooks@gmail.com

Laser Typeset at
Arpit Printographers, Delhi 110 032

Printed at
D.K. Fine Art Press, Delhi 110 052

PRELUDE AND ACKNOWLEDGMENTS

One who did sow and labour,
Fills his barn with grain.

Jalāl ad-Dīn Rumi

Every philosophy starts with the words: "Read, read, read, in the name of reason and freedom, read." I dedicate this book to this great thought.

Reason (*Vernunft*) in the philosophy of Hegel, not only thinks conceptually, but thinks in terms of world freedom. In all great philosophies, *freedom as thinking reason*, stands at the centre of philosophical reasoning. In ancient Iran this rule of reason appeared as Ahura Mazda. While traditionally Ahura Mazda is translated as the "Lord of Wisdom", a Hegelian twist translates this as the "rule of reason". Later Ahura Mazda mutated and became Allah. It seemed that the revolution of the rule of reason would spread all over the world. But then Ahura Mazda/Allah betrayed its own legacy and got detached itself from the calling (*Beruf*) of world freedom and got caught in the trap of theological dictatorships. Since then, reason and freedom have been perpetually estranged from humanity. One, it seems, cannot talk in the name of estranged freedom. Yet freedom does beckon us all. Philosophy then takes a messianic form, from where the calling (*Beruf*) of the philosophical mission is once again reinstated.

This little book first appeared as the introduction to my edited volume *Challenges for the Indian Left* (with 37 chapters) where scholars penned their thoughts on the problems and future of Marxism. Now it is felt that this introduction needs to appear in separate form. As a separate text, it is hoped that the burning issues of Marxism are addressed where 20th century official Marxism can be purged from its alien forms. It is necessary that Marxism goes thought this purgatory where it can cleanse itself from the crimes done by its followers, crimes done in the name of Marx himself. And coming out from this purgatory, Marxism appears in human form.

But not only has Marxism to go through this humanising purgatory, we all need to go through it. Almost all institutions in the recent past have taken the names of reason and freedom and created the foulest dictatorships in their very names. It is hoped that all spurious reasons and freedoms can be purged away, so that real reason and freedom can emerge. That is why we say that this spurious reason and freedom can only say in the words of Goethe which Marx liked quoting:

Sollte these Qual uns quälen
Da sie unsre Lust vermehrt,
Hat nicht myriaden Seelen
Timur's Herrschaft aufgezehrt?

Should this torture then torment us
Since it brings us greater pleasure?
Were not through the rule of Timur
Souls devoured without measure?[1]

Timur, one must note, is not only the historical figure of the alleged barbarian who after plundering Iran ransacked a greater part of North India. Timur is everywhere, more often than naught, not in the dress of the barbarian, but in the makeup of the liberal democrat. But if Timur is everywhere, so are reason and freedom everywhere. I would like to thank all the proponents of reason and freedom all over the world, especially at the Indian Institute of Education, Pune; just as I curse all the Timurs of the world. Many thanks also to the Indian Council of Social Science Research, New Delhi, which has been consistent in pursuing social science research. It is hoped that with the development of the sciences, the specter and reality of Timur will be exorcized. The Indian Council of Social Science Research, by the way, was started by the legendary humanist educationist J.P. Naik who was also the founder of the Indian Institute of Education. The Timurs of India have tried their best to tear both these apart. They have also thought that like Timur they can ransack the Indian Institute of Education. But just as Timur was chased away, and lives only as a nightmare, or sometimes as in tragic poetic couplets, it is also felt that the Indian Timurs would be chased away and would meet the same fate as the original Timur.

The death of Timur is the birth of reason and freedom. This, we say in the name of reason and freedom.

NOTE

1. Karl Marx,'The British Rule in India', in *On Colonialism* (Moscow: Progress Publishers, 1976), pp. 40-41.

IN THE NAME OF MARX

What avails lamentation in the face of historical necessity?

–Karl Marx

When we are victorious on a world scale I think we shall use gold for the purpose of building lavatories in the streets of some of the largest cities of the world. This would be the most "just" and most educational way of utilising gold for the benefit of generations. *–V.I. Lenin*

In the USSR, violence and deception are official, and humanity is in daily life. In the democracies, on the other hand, the principles are umane, but deception and violence are found in practice. Beyond that, propaganda has a field day. *–Maurice Merleau-Ponty*

In short, what the sensitive liberals want is a decaffeinated revolution, a revolution which doesn't smell of a revolution. Francois Furet and others thus try to deprive the French Revolution of its status as the founding event of modern democracy, relegating it to a historical anomaly: there was a historical necessity to assert the modern principles of personal freedom, etc., but, as the English example demonstrates, the same could have been much more efficiently achieved in a more peaceful way. Radicals are, on the contrary, possessed by what Alain Badiou called the "passion of the Real": if you say A—equality, human rights and freedoms—you should not shirk from its consequences and gather the courage to say B—the terror needed to really defend and assert the A. *–Slavoj Žižek*

Introduction

From the above four quotes it is clear that there is a difference between Revolutionary Marxism and revisionism, between a Revolution with a Revolution and a Revolution without a Revolution. The decaffeinated revolution that Slavoj Žižek mentions is revolution, true, but a Revolution without a Revolution. One main reason for the crumbling of the Soviet Union is that it was built on the edifice of a decaffeinated revolution, a revolution that was perfected by Stalin, a perfection carried on from Khrushchev to Gorbachev.

Unfortunately despite tomes written on the Russian Revolution from John Reed's *Ten Days that Shook the World* to Isaac Deutscher's Trotsky trilogy and the biography of Stalin, Simone Pirani's *The Russian Revolution in Retreat: 1920-24. Soviet Workers and the New Communist Elite* and Alexander Rabinowitch's 1976 classic *The Bolsheviks Come to Power: The Revolution of 1917 in Petrograd* followed in 2007 by *The Bolsheviks in Power: The First Year of Soviet Rule in Petrograd*, the path taken by the 1917 Revolution from insurrection to collapse was not taken seriously from the epistemic vantage point that differentiates the two types of revolutions that I just mentioned.

If world history, as it seems, did not make this distinction between the two types of revolutions, in India it was only the ideology of the decaffeinated revolution that had gripped the minds of the party elites. And when in the late 1960s from pressure of the revolutionary cadre, the spark that was to start a prairie fire was ignited; it was once again the decaffeinated revolution that came on the scene of Indian history. For one, the courage to seize power was lacking by the party elites in the history of the communist movement in India. There has been from its inception the mortal fear of these party elites of a real revolution, or should one say in the language of Jacques Lacan and Slavoj Žižek the *Real*

Revolution or the *Real of the Revolution*. In a way Žižek is correct when he says the following:

> Radicals are, on the contrary, possessed by what Alain Badiou called the "passion of the Real": if you say A—equality, human rights and freedoms—you should not shirk from its consequences and gather the courage to say B—the terror needed to really defend and assert the A.[1]

Unfortunately this courage to defend the revolution was always lacking by the Indian party elites. But then the courage to start the revolution has also been lacking. But it was not mere courage that the communist elites lacked. It was also a scientific understanding of Marxism which they lacked. It is thus to this scientific understanding that one turns attention to.

Asiatic Mode of Production and the Rethinking of the Indian Revolution

"The fundamental and most stable feature of Russian history", so Leon Trotsky says in his monumental *The History of the Russian Revolution*, "is the slow tempo of her development, with the economic backwardness, primitiveness of social forms and low level of culture resulting from it".[2] One could replace the words "Russian history" with "Indian history". The pictures of Russian and Indian histories would be uncannily alike. In India, however, on this very economic backwardness, rose the entire ideological superstructure whose ultimate goal, so we have been told, is Moksha. The formlessness of this cultural superstructure was a reflection of the formlessness of class relations. And behind this formlessness of class relations would stand the Asiatic mode of production and the Indian caste system.

In order to understand the formlessness of class relations within the Asiatic mode of production, it is necessary to look at this mode itself. For the time being I shall denote the Asiatic mode of production in the following simple points. It is important to understand that Indian liberal democracy and capitalism in India have grown from the edifice of the Asiatic mode of production. Not only have liberal democracy and capitalism emerged from the Asiatic mode of production, but also the decaffeinated revolution and fascism triumphant have roots in this mode of production.

In the context of the Indian mode of production—whether India is to be classified as capitalist ripe for the Communist Revolution, or on the contrary whether India is semi-feudal, semi-colonial suited for the New Democratic Revolution or People's Democratic Revolution (the line held by the Indian Maoists, following Mao's idea of *Bloc of Four Social Classes* where the proletariat in alliance with the peasantry, middle class and the national bourgeoisie would lead the revolution)—it is necessary to have a short note on Marx's own ideas of class and class struggle. And since it is said that class struggle is the bearer of the Communist Revolution, it is important to understand what class struggle means in the Marxist repertoire. It is also important to understand what the character of class is in the Asiatic mode of production and why the formlessness of class and the domination of the caste system with its fetish for rank worship have led to the triumph of fascism in India. What is important to understand here is the nature of social formations in India and whether class relations are present in Indian history and what type of class relations are there, and when and how class relations have developed. Simply copying what Lenin and Mao said on class (the usual practice of Indian comrades) will not do.

Remember that for Marx the single most important criteria for the understanding of class is that in the material production of life, people get into *relation* with one another and living as Marx says in "similar conditions", that "separate their mode of life, their interests and their culture from those of other classes, and put them in *hostile opposition* (my insertion, M.J.) to the latter".[3] It is then that "they form a class".[4] Living in isolation "without entering into manifold relations with one another" where "their mode of production isolates them from one another instead of bringing them into mutual intercourse"[5] does not lead to class formation. And if only "local interconnections" exist and "their interest begets no community, no national bond and no political organisation among them, they do not form a class".[6]

The question, then is, that would India dominated by caste (and its social organism of isolation and separation), be ripe for class struggle and the Communist Revolution? Or would the Communist Revolution in India be theorised from a perspective different from that already theorised? My argument is that the Asiatic mode of production offers another perspective on the nature of revolution in India, a revolution that cannot be predicated on the revolutions that took place in the 20th century.

It is with this noting of class and another perspective of revolution in India that I turn to the question of the Asiatic mode of production. I base my reading of the Asiatic mode of production on three grounds:

1. The state as sovereign. Here the state is understood as the sovereign and as the sovereign takes the form of what Marx calls the "absolute landlord".[7]
2. The caste mode of production, where the Caste Overlord is the sovereign. Here sovereignty lies with what Marx calls "village corporations" which are defined as "separate communities and republics" and realised as "idyllic republics" based on "slavery and the caste system".[8]
3. The emergence of feudo-capitalism with the advent of British colonialism.

It must be noted that the Asiatic mode of production, or should one say here the Indic-variation of the Asiatic mode, has all these three intrinsically woven both in its economic belly as well as etched in its ideological cranium. These three grounds stand even today. What I shall also say is that the faulty basis for analysing the mode of production—argued in the simple binary: "semi-feudalism or capitalism" (to borrow the repertoire of Alice Throner[9]—lies in the inability to understand the Asiatic mode of production, especially the three grounds that I just outlined.

It is with the question of the state as sovereign and patron that controlled all land and labour activities that I begin the question of the Asiatic mode of production. This Asiatic state, or the Tributary State as Samir Amin calls it headed by a "despot", was involved in economic activity, albeit economic activity largely of an unproductive type in the capitalist sense of the term—*unproductive production*—where surplus was not reabsorbed in the production process (i.e. in the modern context: in the circuit of capital).[10] This mode of production rendered "the expansion of production more or less impossible and reduced the direct produces to the physical minimum of means of subsistence".[11] What happened here is that restricted *productive consumption* took place, meaning that consumption of means of production by labour power and consumption of labour power by capital[12] was (and yet is) stunted. Here surplus produced was not absorbed in the circuit of capital. Instead it was unproductive consumption that took place where the parasitical classes consumed the surplus, stunted the production of surplus as well as repressed the emergence of the entrepreneurial bourgeoisie and the revolutionary proletariat. The formlessness of class relations is situated within this very context.

In the classical formulation of the Asiatic state, economic

production was dependent on the state as sovereign. Surplus in the form of the political economy of the Asiatic mode took the form of tax-rent. The state as tax and rent collector was realised as an Oligarchic state under the guardianship of what Marx calls the "Oriental despot". In India this Oriental despot appears as the "Brahmanical Overlord". As patron it developed (and continuously develops to this day) a patron-client relation that is deeply institutionalised governing entire economic, political, ideological and cultural life-worlds. "Surplus labour", in this mode of production, to quote Marx, "belongs to the higher community (i.e. the Asiatic state, my insertion, M.J.), which exists ultimately as a person, and this surplus labour appears as tribute, etc.…for the exaltation of the unity, partly of the real despots, partly of the imagined clan—being the god".[13]

The distinct feature of this Asiatic state is that besides it being a highly centralised state, is the tax-rent-receiving sovereign despot and as rent-receiving sovereign appears, as Marx says, as the "supreme lord".[14]

Next to this supreme lord stands the caste mode of production with the parasitical castes controlling the economic, social, cultural and political spaces is the second level of the Indian variant of the Asiatic mode of production. The labouring castes are seen as fragmented labour communities in opposition to the parasitical-exploiting castes. The state as Brahmanical Overlord represses the subaltern castes and their life-worlds. Labour is seen as unclean as also the ideology of labour thus giving rise to the manufactured ideology of "spiritualism". This is the necessary part of the sedentary character of Indian history dominated by the caste system. Stagnancy and the ideology of stagnancy, along with the fetishism for hierarchical society based on status groupism and the ideology of rank society, dominate the Indian mode of production. The ideology of stagnancy and the dominance of the Brahmanical castes are expressed in the form of rituals and the suppression of rationality.

The post-colonial mode of production which I call "feudo-capitalism" or "Indian caste-capitalism" where generalised commodity production takes place, combined with the Oligarchic state, based on rank worship and the caste mode of production (albeit modernised in contemporary times). It is important to note that by "feudo-capitalism" one does mean a European type of feudalism. Feudo-capitalism as a part of the Asiatic mode of production is not the same as R.S. Sharma's idea of "Indian feudalism". In feudo-capitalism, the bureaucracy of the modern nation state emerges as a caste group and thus as a political enclosed class dominating the subaltern classes in the forms of State Landlordism and State Monopoly Capitalism. The Managerial Corporate State that is now put in place after the triumph of the Indian fascists will be based on the edifice of the Oligarchic state.

These three points I shall reiterate as the leitmotiv of the Asiatic mode of production—or to be precise the Indic variation of the Asiatic mode. The scientific understanding of the labouring castes is seen within this new mode of production based essentially in the informal and unorganised sectors. These subaltern castes are also seen as the pool of surplus labour and parts of the surplus population. Whether this surplus population is also a part of what Marx calls the Industrial Reserve Army remains to be seen. But these subaltern labouring castes are most certainly like the "great refusal" (to borrow Herbert Marcuse's term), even like the existentialist "hellish other" (that Jean-Paul Sartre pointed out in his works).

To put it briefly and also to locate the subaltern castes within the ambit of the caste mode of production, I am recalling an earlier observation of mine:

> One will consequently have to look at the idea of the Asiatic mode of production from a perspective other than that of both Eurocentrism and the poststructuralist discourses influenced by Edward Said. The 'unchanging' character of pre-capitalist India that Marx talked of is to be seen in three perspectives: (1) that of the economic base where a form of sedentary type of culture arose based on a tributary mode of production, (2) where the Asiatic state because of its heavy investments in irrigation projects absorbed the surplus leaving little room for what Marx calls "productive consumption", thereby suppressing the emergence of a dynamic proto-bourgeois and the development of both cities and the sciences, thus leaving the caste-based agriculture economy and culture dominating the Indian life-world, and (3) the Brahmanical counterrevolution in the realm of ideology that synthesised the above two points in the realms of theology, rituals and ideology.[15]

What one needs to understand is that the Asiatic mode of production was not a mode that existed in some distant past. Instead one needs to see how capitalism grew from its edifice, while retaining the characteristics of the state as sovereign and Caste Overlordship. It is in this new perspective that we shall see the location of the modes of production debate, the relation between pre-capitalist social formations with capitalism, as also the relation between caste and class. It is also in this new perspective that we see how subaltern labouring caste groups become parts of surplus labour where the creation of "subsistence economy" and "informal sector" takes place within contemporary capital accumulation in India. By and large, almost all shadows of the Indian Left have ignored this economic sector, just as they have ignored caste and the reproduction of caste in modern India.

Caste here is not understood merely as primitive division of labour, a view that was held by D.D. Kosambi[16], "but is something more complex", a complexity which continues to thrive in India. And it is this very overdetermined complexity that, by and large, the Indian Left missed out. The linking of caste with modern classes, thus the linking of caste with industrial capitalism and the global accumulation of capital remains the leitmotiv of understanding the nature of revolution in India.

Further the incorrect understanding of the Asiatic mode of production as a legacy of Eurocentric thinking, where an alleged superior Europe sought to theorise on a so-called inferior Asia, has led to disastrous effects. Yet it is important to point out that the Asiatic mode of production is indeed not only the most controversial topic in the social sciences, it is what Brendan O'Leary once called the "most controversial mode of production".[17] What needs to be done is to sort out this controversy. At the very beginning what I will claim is that it is imperative to understand that Marx's idea of the Asiatic mode of production has almost nothing to do with Eurocentric thinking, has nothing thus to do with the 13th century translation of Aristotle's *Politics*, nothing to do with the development of the so-called "science of politics" by Machiavelli. Thus it is imperative to understand that Marx's idea is not to be confused with either the Latin interpretations of Aristotle or with the works of Jean Bodin, Machiavelli and Montesquieu. Nor has one to confuse Marx's idea with that of Richard Jones' analysis of pre-capitalist Asia in his *Essay on the Distribution of Wealth*, though Marx did refer to Jones repeatedly. For Marx, the Asiatic mode of production is not a normative discourse. It is not like Karl Wittfogel's *Oriental Despotism* which drew a fictitious line of demarcation between apparent 'free' societies of the West and an alleged 'totalitarian' Eastern world. Instead the Asiatic mode of production is a specific and concrete mode of production, existing in its own right, following its own internal mechanism. It cannot be reduced to the same mechanisms of slave, feudal and capitalist societies of Western Europe as the Indian Left has wrongly being doing. As we shall see in the course of this introduction, there will be three different structures within the Asiatic mode of production: the centralised Oligarchic state, caste-stratified village communities and communities defying both the state and the caste system.

Remember that the idea that the Asiatic mode of production is a product of the colonial mind is false where a supposed 'mystical and idealist East' stood in contrast to a 'rational and scientific West'. The Asiatic mode of production draws no "imaginary line" (to borrow Edward Said's term)[18]. It does not deal with "the romance, exotic locales, and mystery of 'the marvels of the East'".[19] If the poststructuralist Said was mistaken in his understanding of Marx, so is Irfan Habib mistaken. Because Habib—and remember that Habib is the finest Marxist historian on India—also puts (like Said, but without referring to Said's *Orientalism*) Marx as following Hegelian (thus European) "inherited generalisations"[20] on India, I am taking Habib as the epistemic point of departure to rethink the idea of the Asiatic mode of production as against Habib's observations on Marx.

It must be noted that Marx does not oppose "Oriental despotism" to British freedom, following the imperialist Macaulay, as Habib seems to imply.[21] Note Habib's observations:

> When Marx wrote in 1853 of Indian society before the British conquest, he seems to have taken as his starting point the descriptive elements in Hegel's interpretation of Indian civilisation. 'The Hindoos have no history', Hegel had said, 'no growth expanding into a veritable political condition.' The admitted diffusion of Indian culture had been 'a dumb,

> deedless expansion'. Thus, 'the people of India have achieved no foreign conquests, but have on every occasion been vanquished themselves.' It is essentially this judgment that is repeated by Marx in his well-known passage: 'Indian society has no history, at least no known history. What we call its history is but the history of the successive intruders who founded their empires on the passive basis of that unresisting and unchanging society.'[22]

Also according to Habib, Marx gave:

> ....identical descriptions of the village community for which he quotes *in extenso* from what was probably Hegel's authority as well as a passage from the celebrated Fifth Report of 1812.[23]

Habib's claim is that Hegel mentioning in his *Philosophy of History* of Caste Oligarchy as "the most degrading spiritual serfdom" and Marx's statement in his *British Rule in India* where Hinduism "rendered murder itself a religious rite" were both aspects of Eurocentric imagination.[24] Habib continues, Marx was not "simply repeating Hegel".[25] Instead, according to Habib, "Marx had to begin from such assessments of Indian culture as happened to be the accepted one among the best bourgeois thinkers of his day."[26]

Habib seems to ignore Marx's multilinear theory of history. Subscribing to a great extent to the teleological-unilinear theory of history, the Asiatic mode of production is seen as a "lower position."[27] Habib's reading of Marx's 1859 'Preface' to *A Contribution to the Critique of Political Economy*, where the Asiatic mode of production is recognised, Marx is seen as appearing as "confident that the 'Asiatic' merited a separate place in the classification of the major 'modes of production' in human history."[28] But because of the teleological model of history that Habib seems to give consent to—i.e. history moving from 'low' to 'high'—typical of 19th and 20th century evolution theory, the Asiatic mode of production is seen as a 'low' stage in human development.

There is without doubt no *absolute peculiarity* of the East. The East is no exotic or evil land of tales of either splendour or poverty. Nor is the East caught in an alleged 'low' mode of production. Instead I will talk of "relative peculiarity"[29] based on a concrete analysis of modes of production, economic systems and social formations. Thus instead of the Orientalist thesis that a great abyss of the West that separates itself from the East, I shall mention in Trotsky's terminology as "combined and uneven development" of Europe and Asia.

Being careful about terminology is of great importance. A brief note on Marx's characterisation of the "Oriental despot" is thus necessary. Marx's idea of this "Oriental despot" is not anyway opposed to the free thinking liberal European. As we shall see, Oriental despotism—and here we are talking of the Indian variant of the Asiatic mode of production—is linked almost directly to the Indian caste system and the cunning hegemony of caste oligarchy. Hegel's "cunning of reason" can now be transcribed as the "cunning of the unreason of the Caste Oligarchs".

Consider this celebrated and much quoted passage from Marx where he talks of: "Idyllic village communities, inoffensive though they may appear, had always been the solid foundation of Oriental Despotism, that they had restrained the human mind within the smallest compass, making it the unresisting tool of superstition, enslaving it beneath traditional rules, depriving it of all grandeur and historical energies."[30] Marx also talks of the psychotic character of caste where what he calls "barbarian egotism" concentrates all its energies on "some miserable piece of land" while "quietly witnessing the ruin of empires, the perpetuation of unspeakable cruelties, the massacre of the population of large towns, with no other consideration bestowed upon them than on natural events…".[31] This caste mode of production or this form of the life-world of caste is "undignified, stagnatory, and vegetative".[32] It is realised as the "wild, aimless, unbounded forces of destruction" that "rendered murder itself a religious rite in Hindustan".[33]

And in the age of triumphant fascism where a large section of the Indian population is declared as traitors and terrorists who wage their imaginary and phantasmagorical bloody wars on the even more imagined poor Indian state and the even poorer holy land of India, but in contrast where cows are declared as first citizens; we find how revealing is Marx's 1853 statement where there is a *spectacle* of the fascist barbarians that exhibits human "degradation in the fact that humanity, the sovereign of nature, fell down on his knees in adoration of Hanuman the monkey, and Sabbala, the cow".[34] If in 1853 it was found that humanity was kneeling before monkeys and cows, after 2014 the Indian populace is made to kneel before the fascist barbarians.

Dialectical Reading of the Asiatic Mode of Production: The State and Communes

A further qualification of the Asiatic state is necessary so as not to confuse it with European feudalism. Consider Marx:

> Sovereignty here consists in the ownership of land concentrated on a national scale. But on the other hand, no private ownership of land exists, although there is both private and common possession and use of land.[35]

There is a parallel reading of Engels that we need to consider. The reading of Engels goes through a historical materialist reading. It ought not to be confused with a single-tiered reductionist understanding of this mode of production. As we shall see later, there will be a class of landlords (zamindars) developing as the third tier of Lordship, the first being the state, while the second tier will be Brahmanical Overlordship:

> The absence of landed property is indeed the key to the whole of the East. Therein lies its political and religious history. But how to explain the fact that Orientals never reached the stage of landed property, not even the feudal kind? This is, I think, largely due to the climate, combined with the nature of the land, more especially the great stretches of desert extending from the Sahara right across Arabia, Persia, India and Tartary to the highest of the Asiatic uplands. Here artificial irrigation is the first prerequisite for agriculture, and this is the responsibility either of the communes, the provinces or the central government. In the East, the government has always consisted of 3 departments only: Finance (pillage at home), War (pillage at home and abroad), and *travaux publics*, provision for reproduction. The British government in India has put a somewhat narrower interpretation on nos. 1 and 2 while completely neglecting no. 3, so that Indian agriculture is going to wrack and ruin. Free competition is proving an absolute fiasco there.[36]

The lack of property in land and the inability to create feudal landed property at least till the advent of British colonialism signifies two conflicting arguments. The first argument is that there were communes in Asia (alongside the state as despot and Brahmanical Overlordship), which opens the space of radical collectivity in non-Western societies based on a process of collectivisation and individuation within this collective. The second argument is that there had already developed social divisions based on caste and clans where there was lack of both collectivity and individuality with the dominance of caste, community and state over individuals and subaltern social groups. In the case of the dominance of the caste system, we get formlessness of class relations in Asia—what Marx calls in a different context: a "sack of potatoes"[37]—where a type of formlessness develops that has given rise to fascism. Individuality (not individualism, but individuality as critical subjectivity) here is also related to reason—reason that would be destroyed by the caste system. Marx's argument that the "positing of the individual as worker.... is itself a product of history" would take a different form in Asia.[38]

Here it is important to ask: Is capitalism a necessary stage in history and that communism could only come with the development of capitalism? Or would it be possible to skip the entire capitalist mode of production?" It is in this critique of the absolute necessity of capitalism that we see pre-capitalist communities, as Kevin Anderson says, "as building blocks for an alternative form of modernity".[39] And that is why I am saying that Marx's idea of the Asiatic mode of production should not be read as a static civilisation that has reached its dead end, where colonialism was needed for India to progress. Remember that in 1858, a year after the revolution against British rule in India, Marx writes to Engels, "India is our best ally".[40] In the same letter, Marx is talking of reading Hegel's *Science of Logic* and articulating the dialectical reading of capital accumulation. Marx's idea of the Asiatic mode of production is anti-elite, anti-colonial and anti-Eurocentric. Here I would agree with Anderson that Marx was

> ....suggesting that pre-capitalist Asian societies had been on a different historical trajectory. Moreover, although the Asiatic mode of production was said to be based on a rather static form of community property, Marx no longer saw it as necessarily "despotic" referring also to "democratic" forms of community governance in pre-colonial societies.[41]

"Despotic" and "democratic" governance in the Asiatic mode have to be seen in terms of conflicting social groups—the elites and the subalterns. In more than one sense of the term the stalwarts of the Indian Left (including D.D. Kosambi, R.S. Sharma and Irfan Habib) do not seem to have seen the Asiatic mode of production as an alternative mode of production that provides an alternative path to communism. The reason for this faulty reading in Indian history is that Marx's notes on non-Western societies have been completely ignored by the Indian Left. Anderson says that Marx's *Ethnological Notebooks* in the period 1879-82 comprise 90,000 words on the Indian subcontinent.[42] The Indian Left seems to have been oblivious to this section of Marx's repertoire. Anderson further says that a large part of these *Notebooks* for Marx "have yet to be published".[43]

What is clear from Marx's writings based on Maxim Kovalevsky's 1879 *Communal Landownership* and Robert Sewell's 1870 *Analytic History of India* that Indian society "from below"—i.e. the society of the artisans, craftsmen and peasants—was far from static. The idea of "stagnant Asia" is seen from the perspective of the critique of the ruling elite. It is not on stagnancy in economic production, but changes in forms of commune property relations—from "clan or kin-based communities to village communities not organised on kinship that periodically divided the common land on an equal basis"[44]—that Marx's subaltern historiography points out. One also finds in Marx's writings "social antagonisms… within the non-kinship based rural commune."[45] This dynamic of Indian history has to be noted. Unfortunately post-Kovalevsky and post-Marx, the history of communes in pre-capitalist India has yet to be written. The obsession with capitalist modernity and with European ideological thinking has made the ideas of private property and capitalism as timeless fetishes. For Marx, the capitalism which he analyses in *Capital* was the history of capitalism as it emerged in Western Europe. In "England alone", as Marx says, "which we take as our example has it the classical form."[46] Marx says that England serves as the "classical ground"[47] for the development of his ideas. But there are also other grounds, from the non-capitalist basis—a feature that he keeps central to his *Ethnological Notebooks*—which serves as an alternative path in historical studies. What happens is that these alternative paths meet. What is to be noted is the character of this meeting place. Would it be brutal capitalism being thrust on the non-capitalist world? Or would it imply that revolutions start not from the capitalist world, but from the margins of capitalism, revolutions that should ignite also revolutions in Europe and North America?

The point is to understand the nature of the revolutionary subject emerging in different cultures. What happens in India is that the caste system would crush all forms of rebellion, since it would also crush the ideas of individuality, collectivity and critical thinking. After all it is important to note that the "crisis of reason" to recall Max Horkheimer, "is manifested in the crisis of the individual".[48] It is in this context of alternative histories and alternatives forms of property—especially with the idea of no property of land in Asia—that I claim that since there are accusations against Marx that the idea of no property of land in Asia was false (thereby falsifying Marx's idea of the Asiatic mode of production and arguing for a unilinear theory of history combined with the idea of "Indian feudalism"), it is imperative to state that Marx made no generalised statements of "no property in land" in Asia. For instance in his 1853 letter to Engels, Marx talks of property in land in South India.[49] It is imperative to understand how private property developed in India, how Manu's laws and Brahmanism were instituionalised in the development of private property and how caste and caste alliances dominated the history of the development of private property. What is important to understand is that the state as sovereign with highly centralised powers differentiated state power in Asia from Medieval Europe. What is also important is to differentiate property relations and classes emanating thereon from the European model of class formation.

There are a number of points that one needs to note on the *specificity* of Indian history. For one, it has been noted that the Asiatic state did not emerge from class contradictions (a point that Irfan Habib critiques), but emerged as a bureaucratic elite which was itself part of an economic system[50]. Secondly, concentration of power was *not merely* on economic differences, but *primarily* on social ones built on the principle of social stratification[51]. The absence of private property in the West European sense and the lack of individuation led to the *'civilisational' lethargy*, an *Asian Confucianism*, which impeded economic and political development[52]. But this does not mean that private property *as such* did not exist in India. Note what Marx once said about the emergence of private property with the dominance of the Brahmanical priest class:

> The priestly *pack* thus plays a *central* role in the process of individualisation of family property. The chief sign of undivided family property is its inalienability. In order to get this property, the legislation, which is developed under Brahman influence, must attack this bastion more and more... (What we find in India is, my insertion, M.J.) that gifts to the priest first, precede every other mode of alienation of immovable property.[53]

It is this character of the dominance of the priestly class as Brahmanical Overlords that is directly related to the second tier of the Asiatic mode of production, namely the emergence of Caste Overlordship. At this point it is important to note that the idea of Brahmanical Overlordship is not to be seen as existing in some remote past, or only with political reactionaries. It is something so deeply woven in Indian society that not only the liberal, but even the Indian communists were and are unfortunately yet seduced by it.

Just look at the top brass of the Indian Left and you will find the Brahmanical Overlords—though dressed as one must confess in the uniform of Josef Stalin.

"Scratch a Russian Communist", so Lenin said in 1919 "and you will find a Great Russian Chauvinist". How true these words seem for India! The words however could be rewritten as: "Scratch an Indian party elite and you will find the soul of the Brahmanical Overlord residing in his unfortunate breast." To illustrate, note a recent textbook of the Communist Party of India (CPI) written by Anil Rajimwale. Note how this *A Brief History of the CPI: Through the Party Congresses* locates the legacy of the Indian communist movement in Swami Vivekananda, Bal Gangadhar Tilak and Lala Lajpat Rai.[54] This ideology of Brahmanical Overlordship is based on ritualistic and elitist ideology which promotes nothing but stagnancy. This is how I am reworking on Marx's idea of stagnancy.

To come to the main features of this stagnancy, let us reflect on "stagnant Asiatic despotism"[55] which is said to be based on:

> ...two circumstances which supplement each other: 1). The public works were the business of the central government, 2). besides, this the whole empire was divided into villages, each of which possessed a completely separate organisation and formed a little world in itself.[56]

What I am claiming is that this two-tiered structure is what Louis Althusser would call "structure in dominance" or the *structure of the dominant classes*. This structure of the dominant classes cannot be confused with a civilisational reading of Asia.

Further: village society dominated by the caste system was (and yet is) controlled "village corporations"[57]—the Panchayats—while the "zamindars and talukdars were nothing but officers of the Government, appointed to look after, to collect, and to pay over the prince the assessment due from the village."[58] The zamindars were the "middlemen"[59] who took the form of "feudal landholders[60], while the state is seen as the "sole proprietor".[61] "Real communities" in this Asiatic mode are only "hereditary possessors".[62] This is what Irfan Habib calls, "State Landlordism".[63] After the 1793 permanent settlement of Lord Cornwallis a class of zamindars was created who would cease being sole tax collectors for the Mughal state. These zamindars would be the New Landlords. To quote Kevin Anderson:

> Cornwallis' "permanent settlement" of 1793, which made the *zamindars,* formerly hereditary tax farmers for the Mughal Empire, into landlords. The *zamindars* therefore gained unrestricted capitalist-style ownership over the areas they had formerly only taxed, including the right to evict those who were their tenants, the *ryots,* and the right to pass down these new acquisitions to their heirs.[64]

What happens here is that this legacy of State Landlordism, Caste Overlordship and New Landlordism is inherited by modern India. The subaltern labouring castes became clients of this State Landlordism, Caste Overlordship and New Landlordism. *They were left on the peripheries of village society in pre-capitalist India, and in contemporary times are left on the peripheries of both village society and civil society.* Here it is important to note what Ambedkar said about the village:

> I hold that these village republics have been the ruination of India. I am therefore surprised that those who condemn provincialism and communalism should come forward as champions of the village. What is the village but a sink of localism, a den of ignorance, narrow-mindedness and communalism? I am glad that the Draft Constitution has discarded the village and adopted the individual as its unit.[65]

In contemporary neoliberal times, the den of ignorance along with landlordism remains. What happens is that the character of the state takes the form of the Managerial Corporate State, but this form of Managerial Corporate State reiterates the totalitarian form of the classical Indian variant of the Asiatic state. Bureaucracy and rank worship, essential factors of the Asiatic state, also appear as the essences of the modern Indian state. Unlike feudalism in Europe that gave birth to a proto-bourgeois from the wombs of the artisan classes, the economic and cultural repression of the artisans (mainly classified as unclean-untouchables through the rituality of Brahmanical-Hindu religion as "religion from above"), did not give rise to the radical anti-feudal bourgeoisie.

Pre-capitalist Societies and the Question of "Direct Socialism"

In contrast to both the Orientalists who imagined India to be a part of the 'low' culture of development and also in contrast to the teleological theoreticians who worked with concocted ideas of evolution, I am talking of complex histories within the Asiatic mode of production and the possibilities of "direct socialism" for the Asiatic mode of production, i.e. a direct jump skipping the entire capitalist mode of production. What I am saying is that there is a genre called "Marx's late writings on non-Western societies" which have largely not been recognised by the Left in India. And this is despite Theodor Shanin's *Late Marx and the Russian Road* and Kevin Anderson's *Marx at the Margins.* What needs to be understood is that there are different perspectives argued for understanding social formations in non-European societies and these different perspectives are from a non-European viewpoint. And because of the lack of articulating this very important aspect of Marxism, the tendency to understand non-European societies came from the Mao-inspired articulation of agrarian societies which missed out Marx's important contributions as he had envisaged in his *Ethnological Notebooks*, a work that was published only partially and only for the first time in 1974 by Lawrence Krader. Even stalwarts of Indian history like Habib have said that these Notebooks are "not available to me".[66] The impression one got of Marx's understanding of India was only from his articles in the *New York Tribune* from 1853-1861 and the Marx-Engels correspondence (1852-62) and that too from the faulty thinking that I outlined in the previous section.

The result was that complex social formations and their internal dynamics were missed out. What was missed out was also the dynamics that could lead these societies directly to socialism without going through the process of capitalism. Not much has been said of this form of "direct socialism". A brief note on this is therefore extremely necessary. Writing in 1881, especially after the then Narodniki radical Vera Zasulich had written to Marx about the problems of socialist action in pre-capitalist Russia, Marx had claimed that Russia because of "unique combinations of circumstances" could compel the village commune to discard its primitive features and develop "collective production on a national scale", where one need not go through the "dreadful vicissitudes" of capitalism.[67]

What has been the tragic irony of history is that the very same "dreadful vicissitudes" of capitalism were carried through perfection by Stalin. What also needs being said that even today a large part of the Indian Left have been unable to understand these same "dreadful vicissitudes" of capitalism. In this very ironic situation and inspired by a form of Revolutionary Cynicism one chalks out a path of direct socialism that is able to skip the teleology of these very dreadful vicissitudes. What I am saying is that one should not be obsessed with a form of class-fetishism where only class in a West European type matters and nothing else. In this new reading one proceeds to a non-teleological understanding of history whereby one is able to articulate the idea of "subject positions" instead of the idea of the "vanguard classes". In this new perspective the historical conjuncture of class struggles in India from the perspective of South Asia is sought and thereby one finds both real social formations, as well as finds out how the unity of the Indian *popular classes* is possible.

And it is in this site that one claims that in more than one way the disconnect of the mainstream Political Left from the labouring masses is based on a strange form of spurious theorisation of India, a theorisation that almost misses out Marx's original contributions to the study of non-Western societies. Despite Marx's warnings in 1877 that there could be "no general path of development prescribed for all nations" [68]and that historical materialism did not have a "master-key" to study each and every society,[69] what happened is that even the best scholars theorising on India worked with this general path of development prescribed for all nations governed by the phantasmagorical master-key. Consider the following from Marx's letter to Zasulich where the idea of the iron laws of history is placed in the hermeneutics of suspicion. And because a form of Marxism articulated a theory of the iron laws of history, all history was seen as necessarily going through the process from primitive communism via slave society, feudalism and capitalism to socialism. Note Marx's critique of this point of view:

> One should be on one's guard when reading the histories of primitive communities written by bourgeois historians. They do not stop at anything, even outright distortion. Sir Henry Maine, for example, who was an ardent active supporter of

> the British government in its policy of destroying Indian communes by force, tells us hypocritically that all noble efforts on the part of the government to support these communes were thwarted by the elementary force of these laws! [70]

and

> In my analysis of the origin of capitalist production I stated that its secret lies in the fact that it is based on 'divorcing the producer from the means of production' and that 'the *expropriation of the agricultural producer, of the peasant*, from the soil, is the basis of the whole process. The history of this expropriation, in different countries, assumes different aspects....In England, alone, which we take as our example, has the classical form.' In so doing, I *expressly* limited the 'historical inevitability' of this process to the *countries of Western Europe*.[71]

What happened is that the Left in India could not understand what capitalism in its classical form meant. They also could not understand that Marx implies a limit to the reading of the development of capitalism in Europe, a limit that has to be transcended. Instead the Indian Left has by and large mechanically applied what they thought Marx said in their study of the Indian mode of production. What needs being done is arguing for a new reading of Marx's study of India.

Consider the class-fetishism that the Indian Left suffers from. I shall once again turn to Habib. Habib notes that for Eric Hobsbawn, "the Asiatic system is not yet a class society, or if it is a class society, then it is a primitive form of it."[72] Habib further says, "If no classes then no class struggle."[73] In opposition to this form of class-fetishism I am recalling Engels' 1888 note to the lead sentence from the *Manifesto of the Communist Party*: "The history of all hitherto existing society is the history of class struggles"[74]:

> That is, all *written* history. In 1847, the pre-history of society, the social organisation existing previous to recorded history,

> was all but unknown. Since then Hauxthausen discovered common ownership of land in Russia, Maurer proved it to be the social formation from which all Teutonic races started in history, and by and by village communities were found from India to Ireland. The inner organisation of this primitive communist society was laid bare, in its typical form by Morgan's crowning discovery of the true nature of the *gens* and its relation to the *tribe*. With the dissolution of these primeval communities, society begins to be differentiated into separate and finally antagonist classes.[75]

What needs to be recognised is that besides classes there are also other non-class formations which need critical and scientific exploration. What happens with this new reading of Marx is that not only is the idea of iron laws of history questioned, but also the necessity and inevitability of capitalism is critiqued. Because what happened in the old reading of iron laws of history, is that one had a dislocation of real history from the imagination of the hitherto known Left scholars, such that the most important "moment" (to borrow a term from Hegel) is missed out, namely the moment of class conjunctions and their relation to the Indian caste system. This dislocation would not allow the following: (1) the study of the emergence of the revolutionary proletariat in India, (2) what caste means even today, and (3) what the radical anti-caste thinkers from Jyotiba Phule to Ambedkar meant. This dislocation would not allow a Radical Left imagination of the understanding of the programme of the annihilation of caste and its relation to *direct socialism*.

In this site of direct socialism one says that the stages theory that the Indian Left believes in: namely that a bourgeois democratic revolution has to precede a socialist revolution is as false as the belief that history is an automaton governed by a puppet master. One knows that Walter

Benjamin had critiqued this type of mechanical reasoning. Consider Benjamin:

> The story is told of an automaton constructed in such a way that it could play a winning game of chess, answering each move of an opponent with a countermove. A puppet in Turkish attire and with a hookah in its mouth sat before a chessboard placed on a large table. A system of mirrors created the illusion that this table was transparent from all sides. Actually, a little hunchback who was an expert chess player sat inside and guided the puppet's hand by means of strings. One can imagine a philosophical counterpart to this device. The puppet called 'historical materialism' is to win all the time. It can easily be a match for anyone if it enlists the services of theology, which today, as we know, is wizened and has to keep out of sight.[76]

Since we all know that there is no expert chess player guiding the puppet and since we know that history is no automaton, but comprises real people with real needs, one would have to re-think the idea of Indian history from a Radical Left perspective.

Class Formlessness and Fascism as Political Moksha

Classes, class struggle and class solidarity are, as we all well know, the basis of Marxist science of historical materialism. The formation of proletarian class formation and class solidarity would need what Marx calls "common existence" and "common interest".[77] In India, this commonness would manifest itself not so much as in proletarian class solidarity, as in the brutal antagonism of caste groups built on monopolistic power, rank worship, the upper caste ideology of "labour as outcaste" and a parasitical-authoritarian bureaucracy completely alienated from the masses. Coupled with this caste-bureaucratic system, would be finance capitalism which would now model this Oligarchic state as the Managerial Corporate State.

"An oppressed class", so Marx continues, "is the vital

condition for every society founded on the antagonism of classes".[78] But in India this formlessness of class that we mention and the domination of the caste system would propel an uncanny economic system along with the even more uncanny cultural and ideological superstructure the world has ever known.

Moksha, so we know from this uncanny course of events, has been reached. But not merely individual Moksha, political Moksha. What is Moksha? Moksha is not merely the release from the cycle of birth and death which the priests, sages and professors of philosophy had taught us. It is not a form of spiritual emancipation. It is going beyond good and evil, a going beyond that seek the status of the fascist superman. It is also a form of nihilism that Friedrich Nietzsche had recognised as the sickness of contemporary times.

Why did this happen? Why did the Indian elites have to be obsessed with Moksha and not with reason? It is not merely because the Indian elites built an entire edifice of political manipulation, economic depravity and cultural cynicism. It is because those who thought that Moksha is not only a joke but some form of tragicomedy, those who thought that revolution is an answer to manipulation, depravity and cynicism, would want a decaffeinated revolution, a revolution which does not smell of revolution. But then decaffeinated revolutions could also be forms of counterrevolution. The ugliest face of counterrevolution would soon manifest itself.

Why is this so? It is because instead of revolutionary zeal of internationalism and concrete analysis of concrete conditions (methodological themes that were central to Revolutionary Marxism, themes that made the 1917 Bolshevik Revolution), one had the zeal of revolution dampened with the decaffeinated revolution—the revolution that would only be an imagined revolution. This is despite the heroic struggles that the cadres of the various Communist Parties unleashed and despite their presence in large parts of the country especially in the states of Tripura, West Bengal and Kerala, not to forget the Red Corridor that brings in shivers to the Indian bourgeoisie.

To counter both fascism and the dictatorship of finance capitalism one needs to start from revolutionary grounds that involve the masses at large. And in order to involve the masses at large, one needs the revolutionary humanist method that Marx insisted on especially in his *Economic and Philosophic Manuscripts of 1844*.

Methodologically, thus, one starts, as the authors of *The German Ideology* had said, with real individuals.[79] Combined with these real individuals is the activity and the material conditions of the lives of these individuals.[80] What one calls "concrete analysis" is what comprises this three layer structure of real individuals, their activity and material conditions of life. It is this combine that we would soon know as the mode of production from whence classes and political struggles would emerge. By and large because the Indian comrades could not fuse Marx's philosophy of revolution and humanism with actual practice, they got involved in economic reductionism and went searching from "basic classes", classes that would never appear on the scene of history, or when they were made to appear would go missing like the legendary Missing Imams found in the tales of messianic theology. It is this fact that alienated the Left from the masses. And in this state of *alienated vacuum* created by the Left, the fascist forces entered and occupied this space of *alienated vacuum*. The fascists were all too happy to go to the masses and mould them in the image of the fascist superman. The masses wanted emancipation. The fascists gave them the superman.

The triumph of the fascists in India was because the intellectual legacy of Marxism came to be borrowed from sources where, for historical reasons, many of Marx's original works like the *Economic and Philosophic Manuscripts of 1844*, the *Grundrisse* and the *Ethnological Notebooks* would not be available to both the communist ideologues and the cadre. And when these texts became available to the world at large, these never became part of the political repertoire of the Indian Left. In this context the serious analysis of Marxist philosophy, caste and the Asiatic mode of production combined with the idea of multilinear historicism—the alternative subaltern humanist understanding of non-European history—could not be a part of its programme and methodology. This is also because the Indian Left movement from the 1920s was influenced by the Comintern which by 1928 was in total control of Stalin. The theoretical points of references were Stalin's *Dialectical and Historical Materialism*, *Problems of Leninism* and later *Economic Problems of Socialism in the USSR*. It was this Stalinist ideological problematic—half-baked positivism and half crypto-theology—that would be the master-texts for the early communist movement.[81]

If Marx was referred and used, this was subservient to Stalin's manipulation of Marxism. The idea of the Asiatic mode of production was almost not known to the early comrades. It was only E.M.S. Namboodiripad who once used this, only to have this left in the chambers of forgotten reason. Stalin, it must be noted, had literally banned the debate on the Asiatic mode of production. The reason was that it was thought that the Soviet Union under Stalin had nothing to do with socialism and everything to do with this Asiatic mode. Marx's "Oriental despot" (one essential part of this mode of production) would be found in the character of Stalin. The unfortunate fact is that the Indian Left has not yet recognised this. Marx's *Ethnological Notebooks* (published in 1974) by Lawrence Krader would till date be unread by almost all Marxists. As I said earlier, Habib quite recently said that this text is not available to him.[82] In this sense, it seems to be strange that one wants to theorise on the Marxist idea of Indian history when a substantial text of Marx is unread.

In this sense, the understandings of the contemporary mode of production and the revolutionary classes along with the complex-intermixture of modern classes and the caste system was left almost untouched despite the mode of production debate that emerged in the late 1960s. There are many reasons for this. One is the reliance on the Third International which got totally controlled by the Stalinist bureaucrats who wanted to manipulate world revolutions for their own cunning goals. But the main reason for all these anomalies is that after Lenin's death in 1924 a type of theoretical crisis set into the world communist movement whereby Marxist revolutionary repertoire was replaced by what one can call a duplicate Marxism in the form of Stalinism, where the science of revolution was displaced at best for ideologies of managing and manipulating revolution.

What needs being done in India is creating an alternative understanding of the Indian revolution, where the formlessness of classes is transformed into the formation of a class that is both "in-itself" and "for-itself"—the class that takes on the responsibilities of the revolution. Caste, it is important to note here, is the main reason for the formlessness of socialised proletarian formation. While the Left, by and large, ignored caste, it then started understanding the caste system (informed not so much by Marxism, but by the NGO type of libertarianism) as a form of *différance* (to borrow the language of the postmodernists and deconstructionists), or even as represented as the "poorest of the poor" (to recall Arunndhati Roy)[83], or even as a form of ethnicity working under the rubric of identity politics. Right from its inception the Communist Party of India or the CPI (then undivided) under the leadership of S.A. Dange, Gangadhar Adhikari or B.T. Ranadive never brought the caste system embedded in the Asiatic mode of production into their understanding of Indian economics and politics.

One cannot put the understanding of caste and class in a formal Aristotelian either/or binary. One cannot say: "only class", as the way, by and large the Parliamentary Left has been doing. But one also cannot say: "only caste" as parties based on identity politics do. One has to understand class and caste, as "next door neighbours, and it is only a span that separates the two."[84] The radical difference is that modern classes are fluid and mobile, while the caste system is ossified. India has both these two locked in its unfortunate breast.

It is important to understand that Indian society is a society based on "gradation of castes forming an ascending scale of reverence and a descending scale of contempt"[85], a gradation that has helped the fascists to power. In this case, Indian capitalism has this hierarchical system of lordship and bondage, along with the scale of reverence and contempt, deeply etched in its economic, cultural and ideological cranium. The form of class relations that emerged in India would appear as an "enclosed class" system[86], even as a "gang or clique"[87]. Appearing as "warring groups"[88] and "close corporations"[89], the caste system prevented proletarian class politics to bloom. As the "caste-clan system" and as *clannishness that pervades the dominant economic and political orders,* what bloomed was the not so flowery flower of fascism. In India the flower of fascism would appear in the form of the lotus.

Fascism as Brahmanical Overlordship

While the caste-clan system is generally located as a necessary part of pre-capitalist India, it is also to be understood as a necessary part of capitalist India. The fact that caste also serves as the social, political and ideological forms for fascism in India has to be mentioned.

Modern India could never annihilate the caste system, but re-order it for the purpose of capital accumulation. The idea that capitalism would by its alleged law of history annihilate caste is totally false. Marx's statement that "the country that is more developed industrially only shows, to the less developed, the image of its own future"[90], cannot be interpreted as pre-capitalist social formations disappearing, just as they are said to have disappeared in advanced capitalist countries.

Recall here Rosa Luxemburg's argument that capitalism needs pre-capitalist and sectors in order to re-produce itself.[91] I am extending this argument and saying that Indian capitalism did not and can never annihilate caste. Instead what we say is that capitalism in India (as capitalism of the periphery) reproduces caste. And in turn caste reproduces capitalism in India. But it not only reproduces capitalism, it also reproduces the forms of proto-fascistic and fascistic consciousness. In this sense, the communist revolution and the anti-caste revolutions would have to be *simultaneous* revolutions. All references to the stages theory where a New Democratic Revolution is said to precede a Communist Revolution is totally alien to India.

It is here that the scientific understanding of Brahmanical Overlordship comes in. Brahmanical Overlordship has two historical forms:

1. The per-colonial Overlordship that emerged with Shankara's counterrevolution against Buddhism

where the ideology of social apartheid and the metaphysics of rituality with the dominance of the Vedic life-world was institutionalised, and

2. The colonial form where the Brahmans along with the Orientalists created the fictions of "Hinduism" and the "Aryan race" along with the British attack on the Mughal state, the annexation of Oudh and the creation of an anti-Dalit, anti-Muslim and anti-Persian class of ideological comprador created for the service to the British empire. The present Overlords are this class created by colonialism in the service to capitalism and imperialism.

At this juncture it must be noted that the Indic variation of the Asiatic mode of production is distinct from other Asiatic states, especially the Persian one headed by the centralised Oriental despot. Indian history has witnessed two forms of the Asiatic state: the state model which was taken by the Mughals—i.e. the classical Persian one modelled after the state of the Achaemenian Empire that ruled Iran from 550 BCE to 330 BCE headed by the Oriental despotic "king of kings" (*Shāhān Shāh-ī-Erān*)— and the Indic form of Brahmanical Overlordship with its political economy and ideology of stagnancy. Fascism in India appearing as Brahmanical Overlordship erases all traces of its Persian past. It takes the form of brutal Brahmanism and State Landlordism.

While it is well known that liberal secularism has been oblivious to the questions of fascism and caste, and along with it oblivious to the question and ideas of graded inequality and division of labourers; there is also an alternative understanding of democracy and revolution, ideas that were introduced by B.R. Ambedkar, the great revolutionary, radical democrat and master par excellence of the critique of both caste and capitalism whom both the

Indian liberals and the Indian Marxists inspired by Stalinism (and their reductionist and Eurocentric fetishism of 'class' devoid of concrete analysis) never bothered to understand. This, in a way, would be the biggest challenge for the Indian Left. And since the Indian Left ignored the caste question, their theory of fascism was nothing but the blind mimicking of the Comintern's definition of fascism as the "most terroristic dictatorship of finance capital". Finance capitalism would not be without its brain, soul and flesh. In India all three—the brain, soul and flesh—would be of caste and the fetish of rank worship. What European fascism did was that it attacked not only communism, but also attacked the entire tradition of the European Renaissance and the Enlightenment.

One could say that European Revolutions (especially the French Revolution) could take place only after the Renaissance and the Enlightenment. Likewise one is demanding an Indian Renaissance and Enlightenment. This Renaissance and Enlightenment would have to construct the idea of Marxist humanism, where the demand for a full human life is made the demand of communism. In contrast to this humanism, note the essential anti-humanism in the split personality and culture that Brahmanical Overlordship creates. Note the hierarchical system which is inherent in the Indian social structure. This is what the foundational myth of the so-called great and hoary Indian civilisation that fascism boasts of says:

> The Brahman was his (God's, my insertion, M.J.) mouth,
> of both his arms was the Rājanya made.
> His thighs became the Vaiśya, from his
> feet the Śūdra was produced.[92]

The tragedy is that political democracy in India has not been able to eradicate this anti-democratic mythical culture even in the popular masses despite the great revolutionary movements unleashed since the last few centuries. Instead this anti-democratic character appearing as myth, also appears, to borrow the terminology of Walter Benjamin, as *Trauerspiel* or simply "mourning play". In India this form of mourning appears as a false sense of happiness and as I have said in *Why We Are Not Hindus* also appears in the terminology of Fredric Jameson as the "hysterical sublime". I call this anti-democratic mythical culture that transfigures the sense of mourning into the feeling of false happiness and hysterical sublimity as "fundamental ontology" (following Martin Heidegger's *Being and Time*), where myth replaces scientific reasoning and authoritarianism replaces democracy. The tragedy is that this essential ontological division that the fundamental ontology of Indian civilisation offers is incorporated into the daily life-world. The fascists were triumphant because of this anti-democratic ontological culture. And it is through the use of ritual (as Walter Benjamin reminds us in *The Work of Art in the Age of Mechanical Reproduction*) that this anti-democratic culture is able to reproduce itself, not only as a dominant ideology of the ruling classes, but also as an ideology that the masses have consented to.

In order to understand this anti-democratic mythical culture, let us look at the deep structures of this foundational myth that the Indian fascists boast of. Note that it is one class of people who wield the Ideological State Apparatus. The upper caste elites—the Brahmans—have total monopoly of speaking. The proletarianised Śūdra can only be the feet. What is important to note, that even in modern India, this foundational myth is reflected. The Brahmans who comprise probably 3.5 percentage of the population of India, control the ideological and political apparatus like the bureaucracy, media, educational institutes, etc., along with the merchant class (the Vaiśyas) who fund amply this form of Indian capitalism. One should however point out that the dominant mode of production in India is capitalist of the underdeveloped type that Paul Baran, Andre Gunder Frank and Arghiri Emmanuel reminded us of. It is futile to talk of semi-feudalism and link it to the caste question.

A certain methodological remark is necessary here that locates the political economy of underdevelopment and the culture emanating thereon. India has never had feudalism. Most certainly it did not have a European kind of feudalism. One cannot thrust feudalism as a "universal" category that is applicable to all societies in the world. Instead it is with this Asiatic concept of caste-clan with its ideology of rank worship and bureaucratic overdetermination of the economy that attention must now turn. While Marxist thinkers like Sharad Patil in Maharashtra made a serious study of caste in India, followed by Gail Omvedt, the idea of the Asiatic mode of production that has produced rank worship and the parasitical bureaucracy (which are yet present) was apparently missing from their studies. Patil talked of feudalism, albeit in the modified forms of "feudalism from above" and "feudalism from below". The same error was made earlier by the great historian D.D. Kosambi.

It is in these perspectives of the Asiatic mode of production with its oversize bureaucracy and the political economy of underdevelopment and dependency to capitalism of the "centre" of global capital accumulation that we shall be able to contextualise Indian capitalism and the caste question. *Caste must not be understood as a mere pre-capitalist remnant, but an active part of capital accumulation in India.* It is in this context of the global capital accumulation between the centre (West Europe, North America, Japan, etc.) and the periphery (Africa, large parts of Asia and Latin America) that reproduces caste whereby we understand the extremely important and scientific statement that the Indian working classes have two enemies: the culture and ideology of Brahmanical Overlordship (that is realised as the divided self manifested as cultural schizophrenia which produces economic and cultural stagnation) and capitalism.[93] Indian capitalism is not without its ritualistic, hierarchical and bureaucratic flesh that is rotting with its caste-based odour. Note from the quote from the *Rg Veda* how the upper-caste elites—the Brahman Overlords as the producers of ideology—constitute the "hereditary ruling class".[94] The Brahmans are thus literally the "mouth" of Indian politics and the ideologues of neoliberal capitalism. Since the ideology of Brahmanical Overlordship stays dominant even today in the era of 21st century late capitalism, it is important to look at this very strange ideology. By Brahmanical Overlordship as the fetish for ranking, hierarchy and bureaucratic stagnation, so one means, is "the negation of the spirit of liberty, equality and fraternity. In that sense it is rampant in all classes and is not confined to the Brahmans alone though they have been the originators of it."[95]

A scientific understanding of the Indic variation of the Asiatic mode of production is necessary. For this we turn to Prabhat Patnaik who located the historical materialist understanding of the weaving of caste and rank worship with the downgrading of both labour and the sciences:

> The ideological hegemony of Brahmanism contributed to the stagnation of Indian society, not just by preventing a revolt of the exploited classes; it did so in another way as well, which E.M.S. Namboodiripad elaborated somehow later, basing himself on the work of the Marxist philosopher, Debiprasad Chattopadhyay. And it was by arresting the growth of science and technology, and hence of the productive forces beyond a point. Chattopadhyay had argued that the triumph of Brahmanism under Adi Shankara represented not only a

> reinforcement of the caste-system in the country, but a demise of science and hence of advances in technology. Paradoxically according to Chattopadhyay, the much celebrated triumph of Adi Shankara was the harbinger of a dark age when India lost the edge it had in scientific advances in mathematics, astronomy and other branches of learning, because of both the ideological and social implications of the triumph of idealism over materialism; and since, as Lenin said in *Materialism and Empirio-Criticism*, a scientist must be a materialist in practice, this represented a setback to science, and hence to technological advance. Socially, since the practitioners of technology, the artisans and craftsmen, were those who typically belonged to the "lower castes", the counterrevolution ushered by Adi Shankara means a social downgrading, and hence implicit devaluing, of technological advances[96].

Brahmanism as the pyramidal model and ruling ideology of India is based on the downgrading of the artisans who were (and yet are) the practitioners of technology along with the downgrading of their scientific practice. Brahmanical Overlordship which defeated the oppressed people and constituted a victory of idealism over materialism laid the fertile ground for the lethargy and sluggishness of Indian civilisation. As a schizophrenic Frankenstein-like fetish that has now been given life of its own, it is ruling over people. We find this schizophrenic character when we understand that Brahmanical Overlordship "pervades everywhere and…regulates the thoughts and deeds of all classes…"[97] It becomes (to borrow Trotsky's term from a different context) "messianism of backwardness".[98]

What happened in these circumstances is that the emergence of a radical bourgeois was suppressed that would challenge the Asiatic caste-clan system. Along with the Asiatic caste-clan system, the dominance of the mercantile and usurious capitalist class also stunted the growth of industrial capitalism, along with the stunting of the growth of the socialised proletariat. What happened in South Asia is the emergence of a very different kind of bourgeoisie from that of the emergence of the West European bourgeoisie. In Europe, liberalism and the spirit of Protestant ethics, as the guiding doctrine of the bourgeoisie, emerged as a new ideology to meet the needs of a new world of rising capitalism. Here privilege and status were replaced by the celebrated theory of social contract which served as the judicial foundation of society. Science not only replaced religion as the dominant factor in giving shape to social ideas, but also delegitimised religion. In the Indian subcontinent the new order even post-1947 could not get rid of the old order, where caste as *status groupism* stunted economic and cultural growth.

If one puts the caste system in the Marxist perspective, the first three castes comprise various sections of the bourgeoisie, while the last is the Indian working class. Capital, landed property and the wages system, along with state power would be ordered according to caste hierarchy and caste alliances. But a simple reduction of the caste system into the modern class one may not exactly be a scientific idea. The relation is mediated by a very complex dialectic. What happens in India is that not only is the upper-caste elite struck by this uncanny caste-clan system, but also the modern proletariat is afflicted by this system which inhibits the formation of a vanguard proletariat (the celebrated *"for itself" proletariat* that Marx talks of in *The Poverty of Philosophy* in his typical Hegelese) that becomes a revolutionary force. And because of the principle of graded inequality, the various sub-castes in the last caste also fight amongst themselves for a superior status, instead of battling directly with the ruling elite. Caste also inculcates a sense of neurosis-psychosis. It is the Indian fascists who recognise caste as neurosis-psychosis and mobilise this for their violent politics.

The radical idea of the *annihilation of caste* was turned by them into the ideology of the *perfection of caste*. These issues neither liberal secularism nor the dominant trend in the Indian Left that has been seduced by Stalinism has ever recognised.

In order to understand the nuances of caste we claim that the system of caste is to be understood as:

1. Enclosed, ossified and petrified class that is reified as a closed clan system with its parasitical bureaucratic system. As "semi-barbarian, semi-civilised communities"[99] they manifest themselves as a clan system, creating the structures of extreme hierarchy and the ideology of rank worship. The totem of purity and the taboo of pollution rule its ideological guidelines, while economic and cultural stagnation are its two main pillars. The principles of graded inequality (where various labouring-subaltern castes are unable to recognise their exploiter, but are themselves graded within themselves unequally) and division of labourers (where within the proletariat class there is a marked internal division based on the ideology of caste-hierarchy)—which are recognised as the main markers of caste society—now are mobilised by fascism. Fascist politics perfects these principles of graded inequality and division of labourers.
2. As racism, albeit of the South Asian variety, where the upper castes are understood as being of higher biological stock and the lower ones considered as inferior. For a certain type of Indian politics, this idea of caste as race forms the leitmotiv of its fascist politics. Both V.D. Savarkar and M.S. Golwalkar, leaders of the Hindu Mahasabha and the RSS respectively, based their right-wing politics on the idea of race and racial superiority.

3. Of neurosis-psychosis which creates cultural and political schizophrenia and the creation of the ideology of neurosis-psychosis and cultural and political schizophrenia. This form of cultural illness and the ideological superstructure which caste creates is unable to generate critical thinking and a democratic culture. The main thing that this new form of cultural illness does is that it breeds the contempt of other social groups. The creation of authoritarian fascist politics is an essential part of neurosis-psychosis.

I am here bringing in the psychoanalytic concepts of neurosis and psychosis and then I am claiming that in late capitalism, neurosis (as the eternal recurrence of the self-same trauma) and psychosis (as the complete withdrawal from reality) reaches a new stage that I call "neurosis-psychosis". In early capitalism neurosis and psychosis were separate phenomena. In late capitalism dictated by finance capitalism, we see a new stage of mental illness called "neurosis-psychosis". Caste in this age of late capitalism perfects this strange phenomena called "neurosis-psychosis". Like the neurotic return of the self-same trauma, caste is negated only to return once again. Marx's celebrated statement that the Indian "self-sufficient communities that constantly reproduce themselves in the same form, and when accidentally destroyed, spring up again on the spot and with the same name"[100] is understood in this neurotic understanding of caste.

That is why I have insisted in my *The New Militants* and *Why We Are Not Hindus* that R.D. Laing's idea of the "divided self" and Theodor Adorno's "general regression of thinking" fits in best in the understanding of caste as "neurosis-psychosis" along with Marx's theory of alienation. The idea of the caste system as "a sort of equilibrium, resulting from a general repulsion and constitutional exclusiveness, resulting between all its members"[101] fits in Marx's theory of alienation, while the idea of the "wild aimless, unbounded forces of destruction"[102], fits in the theory of "neurosis-psychosis".

I shall come to this rather strange combination of class, racism and neurosis-psychosis that has given rise to fascism. What I am saying is that caste combines both the sites of the economic base and the political and ideological superstructure. But along with this theme, I have brought in Marx's problematic of alienation, reification and fetishism that deal with this peculiar form of capitalism in India where caste is not only preserved, but actively reproduced, albeit in modern, capitalistic forms.

What needs being said is that the fascism in India emerged from the cranium of the caste mode of production (with the fetishism of ranking) along with the crisis of capital accumulation. What the caste system does is that as warring gangs it produces the ideology of riots and wars thus creating fascist mass consciousness. In this sense one cannot stick to the old understanding of fascism as merely the "terroristic dictatorship of finance capital" devoid of concrete historical context. One has to understand what this form of terrorism is and how it takes state power. What needs being said is that fascism in India has been triumphant in the matrix of the crisis of capitalism and from the caste-class dialectic where the ideologies and politics of the warrior-priest caste not only is made to rule the roost, but is made literally to grip the masses. The Indian fascists have been able to mobilise the hierarchical caste system where the four enclosed classes: priests (*Brahmans*), warriors (*Kshatriyas*), merchants (*Vaiśyas*) and peasants (*Śūdras*), are joined by the *Ati-Śūdras* (those who are condemned to be outside the caste system). Note the pyramidal model where the workers and peasants are made to stand at the bottom of this anti-democratic pyramid. If one cannot understand this pyramidal model of Indian society, one cannot understand the location and functioning of the dominant castes, the emergence of capitalism and the dictatorship of finance capitalism.

It must be noted that the Indian fascists place at the centre of their violent ideology, the figure of the warrior-priest. One must also note that this caste-based idea of the warrior-priest ideology evoked by the Indian fascists and their contempt for the Indian liberals, especially secular democracy in general and Jawaharlal Nehru and M.K. Gandhi in particular, is because the latter did not believe in this warrior-priest ideology. It must also be noted that it is not merely the case that the Indian fascists borrowed (and continue borrowing) from the Nazis. What is interesting to note is that the Nazis were avid readers of the *Vedas* and the *Gita.* And considering that the *Gita*, as the so-called 'Holy Book' of Hinduism, is being propelled to be the National Book, it also implies that the Democratic Constitution is also in the process of being sidelined. It must be noted that Heinrich Himmler imagined that he was the mythical Hindu 'hero' Arjun and Hitler was Krishna, the ideologist par excellence of the caste system. For Himmler deeds of the most violent type do not harm the inner self. This he learnt from the *Gita*.

Note also how Mathias Tietke the German author of *Yoga in the Third Reich: Concepts, Contrasts, Consequences* talks of how Himmler lectured on reaching the status of "Kshatriyakaste" (the military and ruling elite of ancient India) where salvation (Moksha) is realised through bloody wars. Note also that for Walter Wust—German Orientalist and Nazi ideologue who from 1937 was the President of the Research Institute of the Ahnenerbe (literally "inherited from the forefathers") —Hitler was a "Chakravartin" (Indo-Aryan world emperor). In his speech of Posener, Himmler—influenced by the spirit of the *Gita* where Krishna the hero of the Hindu religion instructs Arjuna to attack his kin and kill them—said that it was the duty of every associate of the Shutzstaffel (SS) to carry out action without pity and without considering any human relationships. In this age of mass yoga, it is important to note how yoga enthusiasts like the German Indologist and SS Capt. Jakob Wilhelm Hauer influenced the Nazis on the Aryan theory of racial superiority. The Nazi order according to Himmler was conceived as a spiritual order—a spirituality that led to the consciousness of the superman—willing to kill without looking at the consequences, killing of relatives and family members not excluded. He demanded that one has to detach oneself from such concepts as "good" and "evil." Moksha is this fascist going beyond good and evil.

Without this understanding, it is impossible to understand the rise of fascism. Why do we say this? We say this because the Indian bourgeois democratic revolution has not been accomplished and can never be accomplished. In this sense the very idea of the bourgeois democratic revolution could be a myth. This is because the bourgeoisie was incapable of being revolutionary any more. In India the bourgeoisie (especially the bania capitalists, the Kshatriya kulaks and upper caste ideologues, along with the political kulaks and the bureaucracy) carried caste within its economic base and ideological cranium. Let us see the picturisation of the haunting ghost and its embedment with the economic structure of society:

> Alongside of modern evils, a whole series of inherited evils oppress us, arising from the passive survival of antiquated modes of production, with their inevitable train of social and political anachronisms. We suffer not only from the living, but from the dead. *Le mort saist le vif!* We are seized by the dead![103]

Look at this ghost of the past that seizes us. This ghost is also a casteist ghost. It is of the Brahmanical Overlord dressed in democratic attire. But beneath all this clothing, the fascist body and mind are found. Of course the liberals could never do anything about this ghost and the return of the Overlord. But the Left was expected to do something. But it was also left dumb to the teeth. What they did was only create ideologies, sometimes also producing ideologies of revolution, just as the utopians always promised heaven on earth. And what did these ideologies of revolution (that are not only indifferent to the science of revolution, but which actively repress this science) do? These ideologies created the framework of an alienated and alien discourse—a form of reified consciousness—whereby the social framework of Indian society and history was actively veiled. And in India the crux of the problem was not able to identify the nature of the dominant mode of production which itself is based on the inability to understand the mechanism and dynamics of Indian history. What the Indian Left did was that it borrowed the unilinear and mechanist idea of history—where history was said to be a march-past from primitive communism via slave society, feudalism and capitalism, finally destined to culminate in communism. R.S. Sharma's theory of "Indian feudalism" and the Indian Left's idea of the New Democratic Revolution are examples of this mechanistic and unilinear theory of history. That this mechanical understanding governed by what Stalin thought to be "iron laws" reminiscent of theology was something that the Indian Left never bothered to consider. And since iron laws of history have never made real political revolutions, and since events are always made by real humans, the Communist Party imagined that it would appear as the messianic representation of these laws of history. Stalin (literally meaning the "man of steel") became the messianic representation of the iron laws of history. History would soon be replaced with messianic tendencies, on the one hand, and contemplation, on the other hand. In the contemporary Left movement, the Maoists represent the messianic tendency, while the Parliamentary Left (that went as the "Left Front") became the contemplative part.

What the dominant trend of the Indian Left did not understand is that Stalin left the legacy of the decaffeinated revolution, a revolution which does not smell of a revolution.

The Triumph of the Indian Fascists

The intensification of the juggernaut of global finance capital and the explosion of global capitalist contradictions in the form of the most recent economic crisis, whilst bringing the Islamic State in Syria and other parts of West Asia, also brought the Bharatiya Janata Party (BJP), the conservative political arm of the RSS to power in the 2014 National Elections. This victory of the Corporate Managerial State is to be seen in the light of not only anti-secular and anti-democratic politics, but also the pro-imperialist leaning of the dominant political narrative. We hear calls of wanting to create what they call the "Hindu Rashtra" or the Hindu nation modelled after the Nazi Third Reich. This is an open threat to Constitutional Democracy in India and the single biggest challenge to the Indian Left.

This creation of a political phantasmagoria of the Hindu Rashtra, first exemplified in V.D. Savarkar's *Essentials of Hindutva*, while anticipating European fascism (it was written in the early 1920s when Mussolini grabbed power in Italy), was based on feudal Europe's idea of Christendom. What Savarkar thought of creating, what he called "Hindudom", was modelled after this feudal European theological idea. The RSS created in 1925 had this model of nationhood right from its inception. If Savarkar was trained with European sensibilities, the RSS's version of the Hindu nation has always been nativist. Their models of governance have been the Peshwas in Maharashtra (1749-1818)—Brahmanical rulers where casteist authoritarianism was both their ideology and social and political practice. The RSS model of society and governance is based on the racist supremacist ideology of German Nazism, along with their Brahmanical supremacist tendency. Now with the rule of Zionist Israel, Zionism (one nation, one people, one language, along with the policy and practice of eliminating minorities) has also crept into its political baggage. Its authoritarian, racist and militarist tendencies have always been at the core of its theory and practice. It has three main opponents: Muslims, Nehruvian secularism and communism.

But the triumph of the fascists has also brought in the importance of Revolutionary Marxism. To deal with global capitalism in crisis and the emergence of fascism, Marxism which was declared dead by the Indian liberals and conservatives (much after Francis Fukuyama's messianic "end of history" thesis) after the collapse of the Soviet Union, suddenly found that this death was a false one and that Marxism was, as if, resurrected. This volume is on this death and resurrection of Marxism. It is also about the problems that the Indian Left have been facing, especially after the retreat in the 2009 National Elections, followed by the loss of the 2011 State Elections in the state of West Bengal and the consequent decimation in the 2014 National Elections. A short note on this decimation and the victory of the fascists is necessary.

The BJP won with 282 seats in these elections (31 per cent of the voters gave them the mandate), while the Congress Party which has ruled India for 52 out of the 67 years after independence got only 44 seats. Other parties which include regional parties got 148 seats. The Left Parties led by the Communist Party of India (Marxist) or the CPI(M) which had a large presence in the states of West Bengal (where they ruled uninterrupted for 34 years from 1977 to 2011) and Kerala got a dismal 10 seats. One of the Left Front parties, the Revolutionary Socialist Party (RSP,) broke from the Left Front to join the Congress led United Democratic Front where it won 1 seat. Only in the state of Tripura did the CPI(M) show its presence where it got 64 per cent of the votes. Of the total 10 seats the Left won, nine were of CPI(M) one of CPI. Six of the seats came from Kerala and two each from Tripura and West Bengal. Thus the total number of seats for the Parliamentary Left which had peaked at 59 in 2004 and came down sharply to 24 in 2009, sank to a mere and extremely insignificant 10 in 2014. Both the liberal democratic Congress Party and the Parliamentary Left got a thorough beating.

But this defeat was constituted in a specific logic where the leaders of the Parliamentary Left have been playing Sancho Panza to the Congress's Don Quixote since independence. A new script of this tragicomedy was written. To defeat the BJP which won in the 1999 National Elections, the Parliamentary Left and the Congress got together as the United Progressive Alliance (UPA). In the period 2004-9 the good Sancho thought that he could influence the even better Don. Conjured programmes were drafted and new methods for the transition to socialism germinated in the minds of the speculative Stalinists. But Don Quixote besides being a liberal democrat whose vision was set on the horizons of the American Empire needed the Left to be thrown off their magnificent liberal ship. Don Quixote signed the forbidden Nuclear Deal with the Yanks and the Left instead of being thrown out of the Yankee ship, themselves jumped into the choppy waters of the imperialist ocean.

Locked Brains or the Prohibition Against Thinking

Actually it was a few years ago that two articles appeared in the *Economic & Political Weekly* penned by Prahbat Patnaik and Javeed Alam on the crisis of Marxism in India. To these two articles Prakash Karat, the then General Secretary of the CPI(M), replied back in the party journal *The Marxist*. It is important to understand that this debate of democratic centralism which emerged in the first years of the 20th century in the Russian Social Democratic Party (RSDLP) and which found a theoretical form in Lenin's *What is to be Done?* is an issue which is a burning one even today. One critique of democratic centralism is the liberal type that relates the Leninist idea of so-called "democratic centralism" with a conspiratorial almost Jacobin type of politics. There were also other critiques based on readings in 20th century Marxism. These critiques evoke Rosa Luxemburg and Trotsky, in their alleged critiques of Leninism. And then there is the Stalinist answer that borders on mere rhetoric. According to this type of rhetoric, initially the petty bourgeois intellectuals criticised democratic centralism. Now it is the party comrades who are in the process of criticising this idea of democratic centralism. Recently Paul Le Blanc in his *Lenin and the Revolutionary Party* brought up the important understanding of democratic centralism. According to Le Banc, "few terms have been so endowed with almost magical connotations, and have been so grotesquely distorted by commentators from almost all points of the political spectrum, as the term is sometimes said to be the essence of Leninism—democratic centralism".[104]

In a telephonic talk with Javeed, I pressed the need for a seminar on the debates surrounding the Left in India. Javeed immediately agreed. But he cautioned me that the party comrades have ceased thinking, in fact locked their process of thinking and given the key to the Politburo. This unfortunate process, that is not to be expected from comrades, has taken place and yet does take place.

In this background one can state that the rigorous scientific method that Marx had outlined in *Capital* where science was to strip the mystical veil and discover (*entdeken*) the rationality of society and history[105] would take a backseat in the Indian Left movement. The reason for this is not because the Left in India did not have intellectuals and communist militants in their ranks. Instead the reason is that the shadow of Stalinism and the ghost of a duplicate Marxism would haunt the Left in India, just as it would haunt the world communist movement.

And yet anyone who is a passionate reader of the Marxist classics would know that labour would serve the makings of humanity—to borrow Engels' term: the "part played by labour in the transition of ape to human"—and that intellectual labour (or to use Louis Althusser's term "theoretical practice") would serve the makings of the world communist revolution. However for the Left in India, the world would always be a small place, dictated by Stalin's notorious "socialism in one country". There are two problems, as we shall see, the generic question of "socialism in one country" and the specific one of "country" or the "national question", that would bring in the question of the nation state.

The issues that would emerge would be: (1) the impossibility of socialism in one country that Marx and Engels recognised and (2) the national question that cannot be reduced only to the history of West Europe and the formation of nation states with their respective bourgeois revolutions. Nation states, after all, do not have to be celebrated. They are made on the spilling of blood. Nation states of course are not natural phenomena. Instead one has to understand that nation states are predicated on the emergence and development of capitalism. This however does not mean that they are predicted on the transcendence of feudalism (to be understood in the dialectic of the transition of feudalism to capitalism) and thus declared progressive. Since there has been no "Indian feudalism", its transcendence is simply a chimera.

One cannot romanticise nation states. In fact the recognition of the subaltern histories of non-Western societies, spanning from West Asia to South Asia which have a common binding that far transcends national boundaries constructed by colonialism. It is this alternative history that we need to bring out, this alternative that binds the subaltern people of Asia.

Besides the challenge of recognising the caste-Asiatic mode of production, one has the challenge of breaking out from the chains of the politics of the nation state for the creation of a genuine internationalism. This genuineness of internationalism is predicated on the formation of the Asian Soviets. This form necessarily involves the breakdown of the colonially constructed borders of India-Pakistan-Bangladesh-Iran-Afghanistan-Iraq-Nepal-Sri Lanka, etc.

The fact that the Parliamentary Left is nationalist (in the very bourgeois sense) one knows for sure. And any discerning reader of Marxism would know that National Socialism was a myth and that there was no possibility of this notorious "socialism in one country" that Stalin advocated since the mid-1920s. The fact that the Indian Left by and large believes to this date in this myth is shocking. And in order to understand that there can be no socialism in one country, let us take Engels' 'Principles of Communism', where to the question: "Will it be possible for the revolution to take place in one country alone?", one understands why Engels answers in one word is: "No".[106] One wonders why the Parliamentary Left has not understood this simple fact:

> Large-scale industry has already brought all the peoples of the earth, and especially the civilised peoples, into such close relation with one another that none is independent of what happens to the others. Further, it has coordinated the social development of all civilised countries to such an extent that in all of them the bourgeoisie and proletariat have become the two decisive classes of society and the struggle between them the main struggle of the day. The communist revolution, therefore, will be not merely a national one; it will take place in all civilised countries simultaneously, that is to say, at least in England, America, France and Germany. It will in each of these countries develop more quickly or more slowly according as one country or the other has a more developed industry, greater wealth, a more significant mass of productive forces. Hence it will go most slowly and will meet most obstacles in Germany; most rapidly and easily in England. It will have a powerful impact on the other countries of the world and will radically alter and accelerate their course of development up to now. It is a universal revolution and so will have universal range.[107]

Somewhat later, in *The Class Struggle in France* Marx chided the French proletariat for imagining that they would be able to "consummate a proletariat revolution within the national walls of France".[108] But this form of internationalism has been alien for the Indian Established Left, just as Marx's slogan "their battle cry must be the Revolution in Permanence"[109] is alien to them. For these revisionists, following the master revisionist Stalin, the idea of the Permanent Revolution was an illusion created by his phantasised enemy Trotsky. Just as Trotsky would become the phantasised and "hated-hellish other" for Stalin, internationalism would become this hellish other for the global Stalinists. The Indian Left would not be left out from this fantasy.

In this sense, internationalism was always removed from

the genre of the Indian Left. Regarding the issues on foreign policy for example (take the case of the relations between Pakistan and India), there is no difference between the policies of the liberal Congress and the Established Left. Forget the very burning questions of the right of people to self-determination whether it is in Kurdistan, Baluchistan, or Kashmir. It is the same nation state that governs the politics and ideology of the bourgeoisie that governs the politics of the Indian Left. In this sense it was the map carved by British colonialism with the Indian nation state forming its contours that would serve as the political cartography of the Indian Left. For the Indian Left it was the Indian nation with its colonial constructed bureaucratic system and the parliamentary state that was to be protected and nurtured, as if, naturally evolving into socialism. Nothing could be more removed from Marx's revolutionary repertoire than this form of petty bourgeois nationalism.

Now consider Stalin's response to Marx's internationalism. For Stalin, contra-Engels: "We have in the main already accomplished such a revolution in one separate country, in our country".[110] Consider Stalin's nationalist rhetoric: "Of course, if Engels were alive, he would not cling to old formula. On the contrary, he would heartily welcome our revolution, and would say: 'To the devil with old formulas! Long live the victorious revolution in the USSR' ".[111] One only wished that the "stubborn empiric" (to borrow Trotsky's term)—Stalin and the global Stalinists—had understood that revolutions are "world-historical"[112], and that revolutions have to be "simultaneous" and "all at once".[113] And if only the stubborn empirics had understood that if revolutions are merely nationalistic, merely local, then "want is made general, and with want the struggle for necessities would begin again, and the old filthy business (of class exploitation, my insertion, M.J.) would be necessarily restored".[114] It is important to note that Marx said this in the mid and late 1840s. What he said then happened in the Soviet Union in 1991. The "filthy business" was necessarily restored. But the Stalinists never understood this in 1991, nor would they ever understand it. In fact what Stalin did not understand, in fact began his school of falsification of Marxism, the Established Left took his myths lock stock and barrel. Marx's revolutionary repertoire would be left completely un-understood, if not totally misunderstood.

It is necessary to understand this Stalinist myth of National Socialism with another myth, namely the myth of socialist commodity production. Since it is this double myth combine which dominates, by and large, the workings of Left parties in India, one needs to understand these myths. And in order to look at the devastation that commodity production creates and how money, capital and exploitation are inherent in commodity production let us look at what Engels once said:

> Once the commodity-producing society has further developed the value form, which is inherent in commodities as such, to the money form, various germs still hidden in value break through to the light of day. The first and most essential effect is the generalisation of the commodity form. Money forces the commodity form even on the objects which have hitherto been produced directly for self-consumption; it drags them into exchange. Thereby the commodity form and money penetrate the internal husbandry of the communities directly associated for production; they break one tie of communion after another, and dissolve the community into a mass of private producers. At first, as can be seen in India, money replaces joint tillage of the soil by individual tillage; at a later stage it puts an end to the common ownership of the tillage area, which still manifests itself in periodical redistribution, by a final division (for example, in the village communities on the Mosel; and it is

> now beginning also in the Russian village communes); finally, it forces the dividing-up of whatever woodland and pasturage is still owned in common. Whatever other causes arising in the development of production are also operating here, money always remains the most powerful means through which their influence is exerted on the communities. And, despite all "laws and administrative regulations", money would with the same natural necessity inevitably break up the Dühring economic commune, if it ever came into existence.[115]

When one understands that "the commodity-form and money penetrate the internal husbandry of the communities directly associated for production; they break one tie of communion after another, and dissolve the community into a mass of private producers", one also understands that the narrative of the collapse of the Soviet Union with its experiments of National Socialism and commodity-socialism was inscribed on its forehead right from the beginning. This is because the Soviet bureaucrats and oligarchs spoke in the language that the utopian socialists spoke in the 19th century. Utopian socialism (whether the type of Pierre Proudhon or Eugene Dühring) want *merely* the just distribution of capitalist wealth. The capitalist mode of production and the inherent contradictions and inequalities would never be examined. Stalin and Mao did exactly that. Look at Stalin's *Economic Problems of Socialism in the USSR* and Mao's *Critique of Soviet Economics* and one will easily decipher the essential revisionist and state capitalist characteristics of both Stalin and Mao. For the Parliamentary Left, it is the political economy of Stalin and Mao that serve as the models for their so-called socialist experiments.

It must be noted that Stalin's *Economic Problems of Socialism in the USSR* of so-called socialist economics institionalised this myth of commodity-socialism. The biggest challenge for the Indian Left is to critique this myth if it needs having a scientific basis. Take Stalin's own question: "Is commodity production a good thing?" Stalin answers: "It is not a bad thing".[116] One needs to combine the myths of National Socialism (of Stalin and Mao) and socialist production (again of Stalin and Mao). But it must be recognised that the theme of commodity-based socialism was not only an error, which though institutionalised by Stalin, also had a voice in his bête noire Trotsky.[117] Mao thought that value is not a relation of production (this is Marx's position,) but a thing. For Mao, value is a thing and a technique and "commodity production will serve socialism quite tamely".[118] Once this confusion is clear—of transforming the idea of value as a relations of production (Marx) to that of technique (Stalin and Mao)—one will be able to recognise the difference between the socialism of Marx and that of Stalin and Mao.

What we saw in 1991 is the spectacle that commodity would not serve socialism. Contra Mao, it would not serve socialism tamely. The taming of the commodity is like Shakespeare's *Taming of the Shrew*. What the tamers of the commodity forget is that commodity production is directly related to class formations, human alienation, the accumulation of capital and the crisis emerging thereon. What one has to remember is that commodity production is related not only to exploitative property relations but also related to the estranged mind and the politics of the repressed unconscious. Like the return of the repressed and "the traditions of all dead generations it weighs like a nightmare on the brains of the living."[119] Stalin had not only forgotten Engels, but Marx too. In contrast to the good commodity of Stalin and Mao, look at the commodity which is represented as the awful magician, theologian and necromantic artist:

> A commodity appears, at first sight, a very trivial thing, and easily understood. Its analysis shows that it is, in reality, a very queer thing, abounding in metaphysical subtleties and theological niceties. So far as it is the value in use, there is nothing mysterious about it, whether we consider it from the point of view that by its properties it is capable of satisfying human wants, or from the point that these properties are the products of human labour. It is clear as noon-day, that man, by his industry, changes the forms of the materials furnished by Nature, in such a way as to make them useful to him. The form of wood, for instance, is altered, by making a table out of it. Yet, for all that, the table continues to be that common, every-day thing, wood. But, so soon as it steps forth as a commodity, it is changed into something transcendent. It not only stands with its feet on the ground, but, in relation to other commodities, it stands on its head, and evolves out of its wooden brain (*Holzkopf*) grotesque ideas, far more wonderful than "table turning ever was" (*viel wunderlicher, als wenn er aus freien Stücken zu tanzen begänne. Man erinnert sich, dass China und die Tische zu tanzen anfingen, als alle übrige Welt still zu stehn schein—pour encourager les autres*)......
>
> In order, therefore, to find an analogy, we must have recourse to the mist-enveloped regions of the religious world. In that world the productions of the human brain appear as independent beings endowed with life and entering into relation both with one another and the human race. So it is in the world of commodities with the production of men's hands. This I call the Fetishism which attaches itself to the products of labour, so soon as they are produced as commodities, and which is therefore inseparable from the production of commodities.[120]

Look at Marx's reference at "table turning", where tables begin to dance (*die Tische zu tanzen anfingen*), or where heads dance (*als wenn er aus freien Stücken zu tanzen begänne*). It must be noted that this dancing of heads and tables is related to the game of evoking of the spirits of the dead. The metaphor of this "table turning" where heads seem to dance was part of the 19th century fad of the European elites who were being involved in occultism, especially by playing with planchets. That is why Marx says that commodity production involves not only theology and metaphysics, but also magic and necromancy.[121] So to the question: "Is commodity production a bad thing?" one has to disagree with Stalin. For commodities involve not only economics, but historical constellations which bind the base and the intellectual superstructure where not only classes and capital are produced and reproduced, but also the fetishism of consciousness and the regression of critical thinking. When one has entered the brave new world of commodity production, then one has also entered the world of the dancing tables and the wooden head (*Holzkopf*) possessed by the spirits of the netherworld.

But there is another part to this narrative of the fetishism of commodities and the dancing tables. In *Why We Are Not Hindus,* I had said that this idea of fetishism and being possessed by alien and dreadful spirits which rule us, one needs to replace the word "commodity" with "Hindu Rashtra". This is what we get after replacing the words:

> The "Hindu Rashtra" appears as, at first sight, a very trivial thing, and easily understood. Its analysis shows that it is in reality, a very queer thing, abounding in metaphysical subtleties and theological niceties. So far as it is value in use, there is nothing mysterious about it.....But so soon as the "Hindu Rashtra" steps forth as a commodity, it is changed into something transcendent. This "Hindu Rashtra" not only stands with its feet on the ground, but, in relation to all other commodities, it stands on its head, and evolves out of its wooden brain grotesque ideas, far more wonderful than "table-turning" ever was.[122]

The triumph of the fascists was a sign of the return of the

dancing tables and wooden heads, dancing tables and wooden heads which have now become totally authoritarian. It was also a sign that the bourgeoisie with their wooden heads and the political elites with their dancing tables no longer need the Established Indian Left to play their role of the welfare commodity producers. After all, the commodities and dancing tables of the bourgeoisie would be more interesting and saleable than the commodities of the Stalin and Mao-inspired Established Left. Bourgeois commodities can dance better than the commodities of the Left.

The destruction of this Parliamentary Left could be said to be grafted in its very beginning, since this logic of 'good' commodity production along with their regular doses of Stalinist authoritarian politics would never leave their ideological parameters. Locked brains can, after all, never think. If Žižek said that liberal democracy perfected the technique of the *Denkverbot* or the "prohibition against thinking", then the Established Left would also fall in this liberal democratic genre. The trap for the Parliamentary Left—Stalinism authoritarianism and liberalism—would sink them into the marketplace where the fascists would be able to get a better price for their wares.

If M.N. Roy, Sultan Ahmed Khan Tarin, Ahmed Husan, Mohammad Shafiq Siddiqui, Rafiq Ahmed, M. Acharya, Evelyn Trent Roy and Rosa Fitingof, as the first fighters of the communist movement in the 1920s, created the possibilities of a vision that went much beyond the ruins of capitalism, the present Established Left could only keep the memories of these leaders as museum pieces. Even S.A. Dange, B.T. Ranadive, P.C. Joshi, E.M.S. Namboodiripad, C. Rajaweshara Rao, P. Sundarayya, Jyoti Basu and Harkishan Surjeet would be converted to memoirs. Locked brains can, after all, have only distant memories and that too frozen memories.

But history does find its dialectical modes of moving forwards. Indian fascism would find opposition clearly from the student movement which would now not be dependent on old modes of thinking. This movement would not bow to old ideas, to old modes of articulating emancipatory politics. They would also not bow to the party leadership. Indian capitalism needed its gravediggers and the celebrators of revolution. It finally found this new light.

The Biggest Challenge: Understanding the Myth of Socialist Commodity Production

But quite often light is replaced with darkness. And in this era of triumphant fascism one cannot afford to get lost in darkness once again. The New Movement will have to recognise this fact. After all, utopias emerge when clear thinking is replaced with good wishes. If, however, strict scientific explanation needs to replace polemics in political economy, the same must be said about strict scientific explanation of the dynamics governing capitalism in particular and history in general.

Let us begin with the main myth—that of socialist commodity production, the myth that tore the Soviet Union into infinite pieces. For Marx, socialism (even in its alleged first stage), as he says in the *Critique of the Gotha Programme*, is not built on commodity production. This for certain reasons is not brought into the manifold of Marxist reasoning. Note what Marx said in 1875:

> Within the co-operative society based on common ownership of the means of production, the producers do not exchange their products; just as little does the labour employed on the products appear here *as the value* of these products, as a material quality possessed by them, since now, in contrast to capitalist society, individual labour no longer exists in an indirect fashion but directly as a component part of total labour. The phrase

> "proceeds of labour", objectionable also today on account of its ambiguity, thus loses all meaning. What we have to deal with here is a communist society, not as it has developed on its own foundations, but, on the contrary, just as it emerges from capitalist society; which is thus in every respect, economically, morally, and intellectually, still stamped with the birthmarks of the old society from whose womb it emerges. Accordingly, the individual producer receives back from society—after the deductions have been made—exactly what he gives to it. What he has given to it is his individual quantum of labour. For example, the social working day consists of the sum of the individual hours of work; the individual labour time of the individual producer is the part of the social working day contributed by him, his share in it. He receives a certificate from society that he has furnished such-and-such an amount of labour (after deducting his labour for the common funds); and with this certificate, he draws from the social stock of means of consumption as much as the same amount of labour cost. The same amount of labour which he has given to society in one form, he receives back in another.[123]

The same is said by Engels in his *Anti-Dühring*. Note Engels:

> From the moment when society enters into possession of the means of production and uses them in direct association for production, the labour of each individual, however varied its specifically useful character may be, becomes at the start and directly social labour. The quantity of social labour contained in a product need not then be established in a *roundabout way* (my emphasis, M.J.); daily experience shows in a direct way how much of it is required on the average. Society can simply calculate how many hours of labour are contained in a steam engine, a bushel of wheat of the last harvest, or a hundred square yards of cloth of a certain quality. It could therefore never occur to it still to express the quantities of labour put into the products, quantities which it will then know directly and in their absolute amounts, in a third product, in a measure which, besides, is only relative, fluctuating, inadequate, though

> formerly unavoidable for lack of a better one, rather than express them in their natural, adequate and absolute measure, *time*. Just as little as it would occur to chemical science still to express atomic weight in a roundabout way, relatively, by means of the hydrogen atom, if it were able to express them absolutely, in their adequate measure, namely in actual weights, in billionths or quadrillionths of a gramme. Hence, on the assumptions we made above, society will not assign values to products. It will not express the simple fact that the hundred square yards of cloth have required for their production, say, a thousand hours of labour in the oblique and meaningless way, stating that they have the *value* of a thousand hours of labour. It is true that even then it will still be necessary for society to know how much labour each article of consumption requires for its production. It will have to arrange its plan of production in accordance with its means of production, which include, in particular, its labour-powers. The useful effects of the various articles of consumption, compared with one another and with the quantities of labour required for their production, will in the end determine the plan. People will be able to manage everything very simply, without the intervention of much-vaunted "value".[124]

Note one does not need this much vaunted "value" in socialism. There is one more very important paragraph of Engels that we need to note and understand:

> The concept of value is the most general and therefore the most comprehensive expression of the economic conditions of commodity production. Consequently, this concept contains the germ, not only of money, but also of all the more developed forms of the production and exchange of commodities. The fact that value is the expression of the social labour contained in the privately produced products itself creates the possibility of a difference arising between this social labour and the private labour contained in these same products. If therefore a private producer continues to produce in the old way, while the social mode of production develops this difference will become

> palpably evident to him. The same result follows when the aggregate of private producers of a particular class of goods produces a quantity of them which exceeds the requirements of society. The fact that the value of a commodity is expressed only in terms of another commodity, and can only be realised in exchange for it, admits of the possibility that the exchange may never take place altogether, or at least may not realise the correct value. Finally, when the specific commodity labour-power appears on the market, its value is determined, like that of any other commodity, by the labour-time socially necessary for its production. The value form of products therefore already contains in embryo the whole capitalist form of production, the antagonism between capitalists and wage-workers, the industrial reserve army, crises. To seek to abolish the capitalist form of production by establishing "true value" is therefore tantamount to attempting to abolish Catholicism by establishing the "true" Pope, or to set up a society in which at last the producers control their product, by consistently carrying into life an economic category which is the most comprehensive expression of the enslavement of the producers by their own product.[125]

Note the last eight words of Engels' sentence: "enslavement of the producers by their own product". This idea of the fetish character of commodity production, where commodities (realised as the value-form, exchange value, money and capital) control people, was totally alien to Stalin and Mao. For how could messiahs be controlled by anyone and anything? Note that for Marx, the commodity besides being a necromantic artist and metaphysician[126] is also a "born leveller and cynic" (*Geborner Leveller und Zyniker*)[127]. In contrast to Marx and Engels, look at what Mao said. According to Mao (and note his extremely unscientific observations):

> There are those who fear commodities. Without exception they fear capitalism, not realising that with the elimination of

> capitalists it is allowable to expand commodity production vastly. We are still backward in commodity production, behind Brazil and India. Commodity production is not an isolated thing. Look at the context: capitalism or socialism. In a capitalist context it is capitalist commodity production. In a socialist context it is socialist commodity production.[128]

And since the Indian Left stubbornly reads only this form of revisionism and since the Indian Left is predicated on the revisionism of socialist commodity production and refuses to look into the deeper structures that Marx and Engels had critiqued, their politics can only be reformist (reforming capitalism by transforming capitalist commodity to so-called socialist commodity production).

This act of completely transcending commodity production, one must note, remains the crux of the problem for Marxists to solve. When one talks of Marxist socialism, one essentially means non-commodity socialism. Ignoring this very important part of Marxism (critique of commodity production and the value-form) and then merely talking of collective and public ownership of means of production merely replaces the Marxist language of the critique of political economy with legalist concepts. The Indian Left not only duplicates the false language of Stalin and Mao. They actually go back to Proudhon and Dühring, forgetting that Marx in *The Poverty of Philosophy* and Engels in *Anti-Dühring* had critiqued both Proudhon and Dühring. What was critiqued by Marx and Engels was taken as the essential repertoire by the Stalinists and Maoists. Note Marx here who says how for Proudhon and the John Gray school of utopian socialism:

> *Goods are to be produced as commodities but not exchanged as commodities*. Gray entrusts the realisation of this pious wish to a national bank. On the one hand, society in the shape of the bank makes the individuals independent of the conditions of

> private exchange, and, on the other hand, it causes them to continue to produce on the basis of private exchange. Although Gray merely wants "to reform" the money evolved by commodity exchange, he is compelled by the intrinsic logic of the subject-matter to repudiate one condition of bourgeois production after another. Thus he turns capital into national capital, and land into national property and if his bank is examined carefully it will be seen that it not only receives commodities with one hand and issues certificates for labour supplied with the other, but that it directs production itself.[129]

What then is this revisionism based on? It is based on the idea of "the degradation of money and the exaltation of commodities" which is expressed as "the essence of socialism."[130] Note also the utopian socialists who have the pious wish for the national bank to oversee how commodity production takes place. If Gray had this fantasy of the national-utopian bank, Stalin and Mao transformed this utopian bank into the even more utopian state which would work as the socialist bank. This I call the essence of utopian revisionism which went from Proudhon and Gray to Stalin and Mao. The Indian Left took over these utopian fantasies. Science, or to be precise Marxist science, would be far from their utopian minds.

Let us note another structure of this revisionist fantasy. Note what Stalin says in his *Economic Problems of Socialism in the USSR*:

> Our commodity production is not of the ordinary type, but a special kind of commodity production. Commodity production without capitalists....[131]

Note two things: (1) Stalin's idea of commodity production without the capitalists which has now become the signature of the Indian Parliamentary Left: *capitalism without the capitalists*, and (2) how Stalin's revisionism (where he decides to abolish Marx's essential ideas) becomes firstly totally absurd and then absolutely authoritarian:

> More, I think that we must also discard certain other concepts taken from Marx's *Capital*—where Marx was concerned with an analysis of capitalism—and artificially applied to our socialist relations. I am referring to such concepts, among others, as "necessary" and "surplus" labour, "necessary" and "surplus" product, "necessary" and "surplus" time. Marx analysed capitalism in order to elucidate the source of exploitation of the working class—surplus value—and to arm the working class, which was bereft of means of production, with an intellectual weapon for the overthrow of capitalism. It is natural that Marx used concepts (categories) which fully corresponded to capitalist relations. But it is strange, to say the least, to use these concepts now, when the working class is not only not bereft of power and means of production, but, on the contrary, is in possession of the power and controls the means of production. Talk of labour power being a commodity, and of "hiring" of workers sounds rather absurd now, under our system: as though the working class, which possesses means of production, hires itself and sells its labour power to itself. It is just as strange to speak now of "necessary" and "surplus" labour: as though, under our conditions, the labour contributed by the workers to society for the extension of production, the promotion of education and public health, the organisation of defence, etc., is not just as necessary to the working class, now in power, as the labour expended to supply the personal needs of the worker and his family.......
>
> I think that our economists should put an end to this incongruity between the old concepts and the new state of affairs in our socialist country, by replacing the old concepts with new ones that correspond to the new situation.
>
> We could tolerate this incongruity for a certain period, but the time has come to put an end to it.[132]

If it becomes clear that Stalin and Mao did indeed tamper and manipulate Marx's essential ideas by replacing Marx's "old concepts" with Stalin's "new ones" which correspond to a "new state of affairs", then it becomes clear that the Marxism that we have inherited is a tampered and manipulated form of Marxism.

Recently Peter Hudis has made the idea of post-commodity production socialism a central problem of his work.[133] "Envisioning socialism", has necessarily to deal with the following questions: "What is socialism?", "Would socialism have commodity production, value, money and consequently the wages system?" For post-Marx socialism, these very important questions remained not merely unanswered, but unasked.

For Marx, there can be no commodity production in socialism. Yet for certain reasons the Indian Left has never bothered to even raise this issue. For them (which includes even the Trotskyites) the Soviet Union was socialist (even "degenerated form" as Trotsky thought it). If then these state capitalist models of Stalin and Mao are the models of socialism, then the Left would very strangely be arguing only for a different model of capitalism. For the Stalinists and Maoists, it is the Yankee model which they find distasteful. So they create their own almost Platonic version (or neo-Platonic version, if you will) of state capitalism and pose it as socialist. At least for the CPI(M) it is the capitalists who are bad (or certain versions of capitalists—crony capitalists). Capitalism is in itself never seriously critiqued. The Stalinist and Maoist versions of capitalism would, of course, be far removed from their thinking radar. In fact these would be the models to be seriously studied and implemented. *Marxism would then become not merely revisionist through and through. It would become counterrevolutionary*. What has not been recognised is that the counterrevolution against socialism will not be raised as much by the White Armies as by the army of cheap commodities.

When Marx says that the same crap occurs once again

in *The German Ideology* and the old filth is restored, he implies that the shit of capitalism occurs once again. One would have to begin once again. But for this one does not only have to wade through Auschwitz and Guantanamo Bay. One has to wade through the lavatories of capitalist unreason.

"The Truth is Out There" or The Lavatory Mode of Production

Sometimes, so Marx once said, one "makes even the lavatory an object of divine law".[134] And it is with this new finding that we make new beginnings. Beginnings are always hard to find. Hegel said so in his *Phenomenology of Mind*. And Marx in the *Grundrisse* said that one necessarily has to begin with solid foundations. One then has to begin with the question of the mode of production in India. For the time being, one will skip the debate that began in the 1960s with Utsa Patnaik, Ashok Rudra, Paresh Chattopadhyay, Amit Bhadhuri, Jairus Banaji and Gail Omvedt. Instead one will need to reflect on a different type of philosophising that Žižek reminded us. According to Žižek there are three types of toilets—the German, French and the Anglo-Saxon[135]. Note how this reminds us in an exactly opposite way of the three sources and components of Marxism: German classical philosophy, French socialism and English political economy.[136] What needs being said is that besides the flush of reason that is contained in dialectical materialism (found in the triad of German classical philosophy, French socialism and English political economy), there is another flush where what Žižek calls "excremental function" and ""excremental excess" are found.[137]

One may however ask: "What does this excrete have to do with the mode of production and how is this type of almost cynical philosophising have to do with understanding the dominant classes and the Left movement in India?" The answer is simple: "Excrete is intrinsically related to commodity production. But it is also related to human alienation". To understand this very fundamental and materialist understanding, let us recall the very first page of *Capital*, Vol. I where Marx uses three German words—*Ding*, *Sache* and *Gegenstand*, all three words indicating the English word "thing"[138]. The commodity is a thing, so Marx says that "satisfies human wants of some sort of another".[139] What one needs to say is that the act of commodity production is an act of alienation. But it is also a type of excreting. Just as humans shit, so they are involved in the production of commodities. Commodities are literally not merely "things", they are shit. And just as in Žižek's readings of the three toilets, the shit shows itself and then disappears, so too in Marx: "Its existence as a material thing is put out of sight"[140]. It is in this sense that we call the capitalist mode of perfection the "lavatory mode of production". This idea of the lavatory mode of production is unleashed on not only the Indian economic and political elites, but also on the foundational myth of Indian caste-civilisation that we highlighted earlier. The foundational myth talks of mouth, arms, belly and feet. Since a number of anatomical parts are silenced, we like Phule's invoking of the creation myth of the caste system in *Slavery* bring in the silenced anatomical parts.

But there is something more in this new mode of production and that is the understanding that in the network of capital flows, capital flowing from North America and West Europe to Asia, Latin America and Africa, capital in being exported is literally shit in the peripheries of capital accumulation. Let us recall Žižek once again:

> In a traditional German lavatory, the hole into which shit disappears after we flush is right at the front, so that shit is first laid out for us to sniff and inspect for traces of illness; in

> the typical French lavatory, on the contrary, the hole is at the back—that is, shit is supposed to disappear as soon as possible; finally, the Anglo-Saxon (English or American) lavatory presents a synthesis, a kind of mediation between these opposite—the basin is full of water, so that the shit floats in it—visible, but not to be inspected. No wonder that in the famous discussion of European lavatories at the beginning of her half-forgotten *Fear of Flying*, Erica Jong mockingly claims that "German toilets are really the key to the horrors of the Third Reich. People who can build toilets like this are capable of anything." It is clear that none of these versions can be accounted for in purely utilitarian terms: each involves a certain ideological perception of how the subject should relate to unpleasant excrement which comes from within our body is clearly discernible—again, for the third time, "the truth is out there".[141]

It is this simple method of anthropological observation: "the truth is out there" which provides us a clue to popularising the question of capitalism and the mode of production in India. What is to be said is that the accumulation of capital is actually an accumulation of shit. We have now what Žižek calls "the rise of 'dead nature'".[142]

So what is this truth which is "out there" and how does one understand the mode of production and the dominant classes in India? For this let us turn to Trotsky. Trotsky writing in his magnum opus *1905* said the following about Russia:

> In Europe 5.4 million square kilometres, in Asia 17.5 million, and a population of 150 million. In this enormous area, all stages of human development: from the primitive savagery of the northern forests, where men eat raw fish and worship trees, to the most modern social relations of the capitalist city, where the Socialist worker regards himself as an active participant in world politics……The most concentrated industry in Europe, based on the most backward agriculture in Europe. The most colossal government in the world, using all the achievements

> of technical progress of its own country. This is the soil on which social classes, grow, live and fight.[143]

In this context the mode of production debate in India about whether India is semi-feudal, capitalist, colonial, etc. ("where men eat raw fish and worship trees", to recall Trotsky once again, "having the most concentrated industry in Europe, based on the most backward agriculture") has truths in every layer of the argument. India, as the elites have said, incorporates everything that the world offers. No wonder what looks like semi-feudalism, semi-capitalism and the colonial mode of production, along with extreme high-tech finance capitalism is found in India.

Lenin (as we noted earlier) wanted to use gold for constructing lavatories.[144] In a sense Lenin's use of gold was to put an end to gold as fetish. But then the German Revolution was defeated. Trotsky's "war communism" gave way to pure survival for the Bolsheviks. The New Economic Policy (NEP) came to replace Trotsky's war communism and the NEP bureaucrats came to replace the Bolsheviks. Gold and all the fetishism attached to it lived on and two notorious characters that Marx had warned in *Capital*, Monsieur Capital and Madame Rent, along with gold too did their "ghost walk as social characters and at the same time as mere things".[145]

Historical Materialism and the Ape with the Skull

"Gold? Yellow, glittering, precious gold?" so Marx said quoting Shakespeare's *Timon of Athens*.[146] Gold is what makes "black white, foul fair, wrong right, base noble, old young, coward valiant."[147] Gold is also what "makes the hoar leprosy adored, place thieves and give them title, knee and approbation, with senators on the bench".[148] For Marx the realisation and perfection of this logic of gold is capitalism and generalised commodity production. Lenin's idea of gold to be used for lavatories is a marker for the brutal barbarism of capitalism and imperialism. Yet it is this magical logic of gold that prevailed, the magical logic that turned the Bolshevik Revolution into the counterrevolution. That a counterrevolution did happen in the Soviet Union one generally recognises. The problem (as we have already stated) is that usually the time of the counterrevolution is situated in 1991. This is wrong. 1991 is only the time for the full manifestation of the counterrevolution. In actuality the counterrevolution took place in 1928. Its effect was lethal. As counterrevolution from "within" (as against a counterrevolution "from the outside"), it disguised itself as the authentic workers' movement. What was born was a duplicate Marxism.

And because of this duplicate Marxism which speaks the voices of nationalism, abstraction and Revolution without a Revolution, one is left with a very ironic image of the revolutionary condition produced. The image is derived from a little statuette titled *Affe mit Schädel* ("Ape with Skull") sculpted by Hugo Rheinhold and gifted by Armand Hammer to Lenin which Lenin kept at his desk at the Kremlin. Not much has been said about this statuette, even less said about its relation with historical materialism. One needs to have a philosophical look at this picture. Let us thus have a look at it.

This little statuette is of an ape, posed in the style of Auguste Rodin's celebrated sculpture "The Thinker". The ape, like Rodin's humanist thinker, is deep in thought. He is sitting on books. Calipers meant for scientific measurement are held with his feet. But this figure is the exact reverse of Rodin's figure. The ape evokes the figure of Shakespeare's Hamlet who mourns the death of his court jester, Yorick. In his hands is a human skull. Amongst the books that he is sitting on, the most visible one is the *Bible* which has *eritis sicut dues* ("ye shall be as gods") written on it. *Eritis sicut dues*, one must note, is from the chapter Genesis in the *Bible*, recalling the temptation of Eve to eat the forbidden fruit from the tree of the knowledge of good and evil, by the snake, the devil himself. Darwin's magnum opus is also seen next to the *Bible*. The narrative of science and theology are intertwined in this statuette.

Now any reader of Marx will recognise that there is some sort of tragicomic dramaturgy found in this rendering. But why did Lenin keep this statuette on his study desk? Did he anticipate the counterrevolution and the complete collapse of the Soviet Union? Does the figure of the contemplating ape signify evolution in the reverse? Or are there other philosophical questions of knowledge, emancipation and power that had also fascinated besides Rheinhold and Goethe, also fascinate Lenin? Was then this ape with the skull nothing but another tragic rendering of European aesthetics akin to Goethe's *Faust*? A historical materialist answer is that Lenin was reminding himself that counterrevolution marches alongside the forces of revolution and history does not move, as if, according to some miraculous law of development.[149]

But this figure of the ape with the skull is not only about tragicomic dramaturgy. It is about the pursuit of knowledge, in fact, about what one may call after Friedrich Nietzsche as the "will to power" or in contrast to Nietzsche, as what Jürgen Habermas calls "knowledge and human interests". In *What is to be Done?*, Lenin had said that "without revolutionary theory there can be no revolutionary movement".[150] But we have a seeming contrasting narrative. In Goethe's magnum opus *Faust* the devil, Mephistopheles seems to be saying that one can have spontaneous revolution without theoretical intervention. Consider Mephistopheles:

> All theory, my friend, is grey,
> But green is life's golden tree.[151]

Now relate this couplet with Rheinhold's statuette and the concealed image of the Biblical tree of knowledge with its forbidden fruits. Goethe's tree (unlike Rheinhold's absent-present tree) is both green and golden. Yet the gold is not Lenin's to be used for constructing lavatories. What Goethe is decrying (as Marx would do later) is the scholastic part of human knowledge (all theory is grey) claiming that scholasticism is basically nothing but pure sterility, and it is better to be tempted by the devil and taste the fruit of the knowledge of good and evil. Mephistopheles, in this sense, is the rebel, unlike Rheinhold's pondering ape who in pure contemplation refuses to partake in the class struggle, or if one remains with the Biblical narrative, then refusing to participate in the struggle between good and evil. Mephistopheles, in this sense, is the philosopher par excellence of the philosophy of praxis. But why did Lenin think it necessary to remind himself of this blundering ape? Why was there no Mephistopheles on his study desk?

Consequently what we see is that the history of 20th century Marxism is based on the struggle between Mephistopheles and the ape, praxis and contemplation, internationalism and nationalism, concreteness and abstractions and Revolution with a Revolution vs. Revolution without a Revolution. History knows Lenin, Trotsky, Rosa Luxemburg, et al. as the Revolutionaries with a Revolution as against the other greats in revolutionary history—Georgi Plekhanov, Eduard Bernstein, Karl Kautsky, Zinoviev—all who were undoubtedly great revolutionaries, but tragically Revolutionaries without the Revolution. They were thus duplicate revolutionaries, revolutionaries that ultimately feared the Revolution. The Established Left has perfected this rather bizarre Revolution without a Revolution.

But there is more to this Revolution without the

Revolution, and that is the counterrevolution against the Leninist theory and praxis of the party (that he had first outlined in his *What is to be Done?* and reaching its climax in *State and Revolution*), a counterrevolution perfected by Stalin, speaking however in the name of Lenin. We noted that a counterrevolution took place against Marx. Now we shall see a counterrevolution against Lenin that speaks in his name. The Indian comrades would, by and large, follow the path given by Stalin. Lenin's revolutionary theme of the dialectics of spontaneity and intellectual work in the masses in his *What is to be Done?* would be totally absent from the understanding on the Indian Left. But there is more to the Stalin question than those of philosophical importance.

On December 24, 1922, an ailing Lenin (he was shot in the head by Dora Kaplan) dictated notes that go as the 'Letter to the Congress' where he says:

> Comrade Stalin, having become Secretary-General, has unlimited authority concentrated in his hands, and I am not sure whether he will always be capable of using that authority with sufficient caution. Comrade Trotsky, on the other hand, as his struggles against the C.C. on the question of the People's Commissariat for Communications has already proved, is distinguished not only by outstanding ability. He is personally perhaps the most capable man in the present C.C., but he has displayed excessive self-assurance and shown excessive preoccupation with the purely administrative side of the work.[152]

Lenin was talking of the dangers of split in the party. But the dangers of a split were not related only to the perception of Stalin as having an authoritarian personality, but related to the understanding of the relation of authoritarianism to the class structure of society. But there is another important question when one is reading this famous 'Letter to the Congress', namely, the question of dialectics. Consider Lenin:

> Speaking of the young C.C. members, I wish to say a few words about Bukharin and Pyatakov. They are, in my opinion, the most outstanding figures (among the younger ones), and the following must be borne in mind about them: Bukharin is not only a most valuable and major theorist of the Party; he is also rightly considered the favourite of the whole Party, but his theoretical views can be classified as fully Marxist only with the great reserve, for there is something scholastic about him (he has never made a study of dialectics, and, I think, never fully appreciated it).[153]

There are two conclusions that one derives from the above quotes, one that Stalin represented authoritarianism of the worst kind (all the comrades that Lenin mentions in the letter were killed by Stalin), and the other concern is the question of dialectics, especially that of Hegelian dialectics and its relation to Marxism that concerned Lenin at least since 1914. But why does one, so the reader may ask, talk of dialectics and Stalin after talking of dramaturgy, when one is talking of the question of Left politics in India? We mention this because it is Stalinism (or if it is not the brutal kind of Stalinism, then it is the marriage of liberalism with Stalinism) and the lack of the understanding of dialectics that remain the core of Established Left politics in India till date.

But one may ask: "What about the Maoists who have been declared as the single biggest security threat by the previous Indian government? Would they also be Stalinists, *or would one have to understand them as Stalinists in rebellion against Stalinism?*" What I shall be doing here in the introduction is drawing the typology of the Indian Stalinists (the Established Left) and the Maoists in the philosophical background of *history that has turned against itself*.

And this revenge of history—history turning itself—is best represented by the triumph of the complete loss of the secular parties in the 2014 National Elections with 282 seats bagged by the BJP. This revenge of history would begin with the end of the rule of the Left Front where their uninterrupted rule for 34 years from 1977 to 2011 would end. The narrative of the collapse in West Bengal, and now down to minuscule numbers in parliament, could be said to be the finale of this tragicomedy. This volume locates the challenges for the Indian Left in this political background.

If Rheinhold's ape is pondering over a human skull sitting on books of theology and science, the question that one can pose is: "Who is the ape and whose skull is in the hands of the ape?" "Is the ape the Indian fascist and the skull that of the Indian Stalinist?" "Or is the ape a Stalinist and the skull that of the toiling masses?" "Or is the ape both a fascist and a Stalinist?"

Stalinism and Indian Stalinism

At this moment it is important to note what Stalinism in the Soviet Union represented and what the Indian Left movement because of its ideological unclarity succumbed to the Stalinist ideological prison house.

By Stalinism one means the following:

1. Counterrevolution in the Soviet Union where the New Economic Policy (NEP) bureaucrats replaced the grassroots communists followed by the massacre of the Old Bolsheviks.
2. Fear of World Revolution and the active attempt to sabotage World Revolution. The massacre of the Shanghai communists by Chiang Kai-shek in 1927 is an example of the fear of the World Revolution. Stalin knew that any revolution would displace the bureaucratic Thermidor. Stalin's role has been infamous in the alliance with the Kuomintang led by Chiang Kai-shek and the consequent suppression of the Chinese Soviets. This is what Stalin in his typical rhetorical way said. Note for him any autonomous

action of the Chinese proletariat was foolish and the Chinese communists had to be appendages of the Kuomintang. Note this Stalinist rhetoric:

Chiang Kai-shek is submitting to discipline. The Kuomintang is a bloc, a sort of revolutionary parliament, with the Right, the Left, and the Communists. Why make a coup d'etat? Why drive away the Right when we have the majority and when the Right listens to us? ... At present, we need the Right. It has capable people, who still direct the army and lead it against the imperialists. Chiang Kai-shek has perhaps no sympathy for the revolution but he is leading the army and cannot do otherwise than lead it against the imperialists. Beside this, the people of the Right have relations with the General Chang Tso-lin [the Manchurian warlord] and understand very well how to demoralise them and to induce them to pass over to the side of the revolution, bag and baggage, without striking a blow. Also, they have connections with the rich merchants and can raise money from them. So they have to be utilised to the end, squeezed out like a lemon, and then flung away.[154]

Note the absurdity of using the rightists and then imaging that the right-wing can be "utilised to the end, squeezed out like a lemon, and then flung away". The next week (April 12, 1927) after Stalin's infamous speech, Chiang Kai-shek ordered his troops on the communists where thousands of the vanguard fighters of the Chinese Revolution were brutally massacred. Stalinism always meant that the proletariat was not yet conscious of its mission, that the time for revolution was "not ripe" and that every revolution was to be predicated on its national bourgeoisie. This effectually meant that every revolution has necessarily to be a decaffeinated revolution, an imagined revolution that never happens.

If the massacre of Chiang Kai-shek in 1927 had a Stalinist hand, the rise of the Nazis in Germany in 1933 was not, as if, Stalin was invisible from the scene. It is not merely the case that the Molotov-Ribbentrop deal (August 23, 1939) was an opportunist deal, or even a brilliant deal (as imagined by the Stalinists). It was a sign of the simultaneity of two counterrevolutions—the fascist one and the Bonapartist-Stalinist one. In 1931 under the influence of Stalin the German Communist Party (KPD) called the Nazis "working people's comrades". It was also not the case that Stalin was a blundering idiot who shifted from the position that social democrats were social fascists (in fact worse that the fascists themselves), to the position of the united front where at the Seventh Congress of the Comintern in 1935, Georgi Dimitrov outlined the new policy of the "popular front".

3. Theological interpretation of Marxism where Marxism was declared a "science" which studies "laws" which "take place independently of the will of man. Man may discover these laws, get to know them, study them, reckon with them in his activities and utilise them in the interest of society, but he cannot change or abolish them".[155] Nothing more absurd could be formulated. Note how this contemplative attitude which Stalin keeps at the basis of his understanding of Marxism is completely in antithesis to Marx's dictum where the point is *to change the world*.[156]

4. Authoritarian state, socialist commodity production and nationalism in antithesis to Marx's stateless society that has necessarily transcended commodity production and national boundaries.

While a large part of the Indian Left inherited the above stated Stalinist baggage, what marks them off is their fetish for bureaucratic empiricism that may not be *actively* counterrevolutionary, but because of its unconscious and unwitting *Stalinist goal of capitalism without the capitalists*, post-Stalin Stalinism (which includes the Parliamentary Left) would be essentially pro-capitalist, nationalist and consequently against internationalism and the praxis of the international proletariat.

To conclude it is necessary to state that the Indian Left has also been married to Nehruvian liberalism. It is these two souls—of Stalin and Nehru—that are locked in the unfortunate breast of the Parliamentary Left. And like Faust they would inevitably be hurled into their capitalist hell.

Method

In the third volume of *Capital*, Marx says that the stripping of the "estranged outward appearance of economic relationships" forms the basis of the dialectical materialist method.[157] Marx adds: "All science would be superfluous if the outward appearance and the essence of things directly coincided"[158] and that the "force of abstraction" would serve as the microscope that would be able to discover the "economic-cell form" of society.[159] What is thus needed is the "microscopic anatomy" of society.[160] And in the Afterword of the first volume of *Capital* Marx says:

> My dialectic method is not only different from the Hegelian, but is its direct opposite. To Hegel, the life process of the human brain, i.e. the process of thinking, which, under the name of "the Idea," he even transforms into an independent subject, is

the demiurgos of the real world, and the real world is only the external, phenomenal form of "the Idea." With me, on the contrary, the ideal is nothing else than the material world reflected by the human mind, and translated into forms of thought.

The mystifying side of Hegelian dialectic I criticised nearly thirty years ago, at a time when it was still the fashion. But just as I was working at the first volume of "Das Kapital," it was the good pleasure of the peevish, arrogant, mediocre Epigonoi who now talk large in cultured Germany, to treat Hegel in same way as the brave Moses Mendelssohn in Lessing's time treated Spinoza, i.e., as a "dead dog." I therefore openly avowed myself the pupil of that mighty thinker, and even here and there, in the chapter on the theory of value, coquetted with the modes of expression peculiar to him. The mystification which dialectic suffers in Hegel's hands, by no means prevents him from being the first to present its general form of working in a comprehensive and conscious manner. With him it is standing on its head. It must be turned right side up again (*umstülpen*), if you would discover (*entdecken*) the rational kernel within the mystical shell.

In its mystified form, dialectic became the fashion in Germany, because it seemed to transfigure and to glorify the existing state of things. In its rational form it is a scandal and abomination to bourgeoisdom and its doctrinaire professors, because it includes in its comprehension and affirmative recognition of the existing state of things, at the same time also, the recognition of the negation of that state, of its inevitable breaking up; because it regards every historically developed social form as in fluid movement, and therefore takes into account its transient nature not less than its momentary existence; because it lets nothing impose upon it, and is in its essence critical and revolutionary.

The contradictions inherent in the movement of capitalist society impress themselves upon the practical bourgeois most strikingly in the changes of the periodic cycle, through which modern industry runs, and whose crowning point is the

> universal crisis. That crisis is once again approaching, although as yet but in its preliminary stage; and by the universality of its theatre and the intensity of its action it will drum dialectics even into the heads of the mushroom-upstarts of the new, holy Prusso-German empire.[161]

But courtesy Stalin and the ape with the skull, the crisis of capitalism led to the decaffeinated revolutions. It is here that we need to understand that "the betrayal of socialism", as Raya Dunayevskaya once said, "came from within the socialist movement."[162] In this case of betrayal, what one needs is a re-emergence of Revolutionary Marxism, that itself needs a creative and activist reimagining of Marxism. Revolutionary Marxism is not reactive like the political practice of our contemporary parliamentary comrades trained in both Brahmanical Overlordship and Eurocentrism.

It was Alvin Gouldner who once said that Marxism has two distinct strains—one is the critical one (following the line of reasoning started by Georg Lukács, Antonio Gramsci and Karl Korsch) and the other the scientific one (namely that of the structuralist school of Louis Althusser)[163]. However in contrast to Gouldner, it needs to be said that Marxist *critique* is not alienated from the realm of *science*, just as *human freedom* is not estranged from *necessity*. Yet what one finds is that the dominant trend in the Indian Left worked on the dualistic space of bourgeois positivism, where science and critique, necessity and freedom are broken as the two unfortunate parts of the Faustean soul.

In contrast to this split between humanism and science that has completely trapped and decimated the Old Left in India, we have Marx's reflections where his 1865 letter to J.B.S. Schweitzer defines science as the "critical knowledge of the historical movement which itself produces the material conditions of emancipation".[164] And in the *Economic and Philosophic Manuscripts of 1844* and in *The German Ideology*

Marx talks of understanding the idea of a unified science, the science of history that has two sides: that of nature and that of humanity.[165] Science, in this sense, is always critical and humanistic.

It is this critical and humanist side of science that we must turn to. One then must close the chapter of what may be called "Old Socialism" in all its revisionist and corrupted forms that haunted the stage of 20th century world history. One can do this when one can drum dialectics not only "into the heads of the mushroom-upstarts of the new, holy Prusso-German empire", but primarily drum dialectics into the heads of the global imperialist empire. It is only then when one can herald a New Socialism. New Socialism recognises that communism is both humanism and naturalism.[166] It also recognises that communism is essentially humanistic and about the "appropriation of the human essence".[167]

Humanity, in this sense, and nothing but humanity, stands at the base of New Socialism. And in the epoch of global economic and environment disaster of apocalyptic proportions, humanity will have to think about its existence as *collective existence*. In this sense it will have to shed its caste, class and and national characteristics.

In this sense of belonging to a large collective, one recalls a philosophical statement that Spinoza espoused: "Neither to weep nor to laugh but to understand". But to understand one has to read, read every text, every sentence, word and letter.

And in this revolutionary sense, one needs to recall a messianic tradition, and tell the comrades:

Read,

Read,

In the name of Marx,

Read.......

NOTES

1. Slavoj Žižek, 'Introduction. Robespierre, or the 'Divine Violence' of Terror', in Maximilen Robespierre, *Virtue and Terror* (London: Verso, 2007), p. VII
2. Leon Trotsky, *The History of the Russian Revolution*, trans. Max Eastman (London: Victor Gollancz Ltd., 1934), p. 25.
3. Karl Marx, 'The Eighteenth Brumaire of Louis Bonaparte', in *Marx. Engels. Selected Works* (Moscow: Progress Publishers, 1975), pp. 170-1.
4. Ibid., p. 171.
5. Ibid., p. 170.
6. Ibid., p. 171.
7. Karl Marx, 'To Frederick Engels, in London' Manchester, June 6, 1853, in *Marx. Engels. Selected Correspondence* (Moscow: Progress Publishers, 1975), p. 80.
8. Ibid.
9. See Alice Thorner, 'Semi-feudalism or Capitalism? Contemporary Debates on Classes and Modes of Production in India', in *Economic & Political Weekly*, December 4, 1982.
10. Remember that when the neoliberals after 1991 called the Indian Nehruvian state a 'socialist' state, it was a misnomer. The Nehruvian state (with its industrial licensing regime) in a certain sense was a continuation of the classical Asian state as sovereign and patron.
11. Karl Marx, *Capital*, Vol. III (Moscow: Progress Publishers, 1986), p. 796.
12. See Karl Marx, *Capital*, Vol. I, trans. Samuel Moore and Edward Aveling (Moscow: Progress Publishers, 1983), pp. 178-9.
13. Karl Marx, *Grundrisse* trans. Martin Nicolas (London: Penguin, 1974), p. 473.
14. Karl Marx, *Capital*, Vol. III, p. 791.
15. See my 'Asiatic Mode of Production, Caste and the Indian Left', in *Economic & Political Weekly*, Vol. XLIX, No. 19, May 10, 2014, p. 44.
16. See D.D. Kosambi *The Culture and Civilisation of Ancient India in Historical Outline* (New Delhi: Vikas Publishing House, 2000), p. 50.

17. Brendan O'Leary, *The Asiatic Mode of Production. Oriental Despotism, Historical Materialism and Indian History* (Oxford: Basil Blackwell, 1989), pp. 7-39.
18. See Edward Said, *The Question of Palestine* (New York: Vintage Books, 1992), p. 3.
19. Ibid.
20. Irfan Habib, 'Marx's Perception of India', in *Karl Marx. On India*, ed. Iqbal Husain (New Delhi: Tulika Books, 2006), pp. XX-XXII.
21. Ibid., p. XXVII, n. 46.
22. Ibid., p. XX.
23. Ibid., p. XXI.
24. Ibid.
25. Ibid.
26. Ibid., pp. XXI-XXII.
27. Ibid., p. XXXIII.
28. Ibid., p. XXI.
29. See Marian Sawer, *Marxism and the Question of the Asiatic Mode of Production* (The Hague: Martinus Nijhoff, 1977), p. 159.
30. Karl Marx, 'The British Rule in India', in *On Colonialism* (Moscow: Progress Publishers, 1976), p. 40.
31. Ibid.
32. Ibid.
33. Ibid.
34. Ibid., pp. 40-41.
35. Ibid.
36. Frederick Engels, 'To Karl Marx in London, Manchester, June 6, 1853', in *Marx. Engels. Collected Works*, Vol. 39 (Moscow: Progress Publishers, 1983), pp. 335-6.
37. Karl Marx, 'The Eighteenth Brumaire of Louis Bonaparte', p. 170.
38. Karl Marx, *Grundrisse*, p. 472.
39. Kevin Anderson, *Not Just Capital and Class: Marx on Non-Western Societies, Nationalism and Ethnicity*, (2010), http///www.internationalmarxisthumanist.org/articles.
40. Karl Marx, 'To Frederick Engels in Manchester', London, January 16, 1858', *Marx. Engels. Collected Works*, Vol. 40

(London: Lawrence and Wishart, 2010), p. 249. See also Kevin Anderson, op.cit.

41. Kevin Anderson, op. cit. Anderson uses the terms "communal property" and "communal governance" which in the Indian context has a reverse meaning. I have replaced the word "communal" with the term "community".
42. Ibid.
43. Ibid.
44. Ibid.
45. Ibid.
46. Karl Marx, *Capital*, Vol. I, p. 670. See also Karl Marx, 'First Draft of the Reply to V.I. Zasulich's Letter', in *Marx. Engels. Selected Works in Three Volumes.* Volume Three (Moscow: Progress Publishers, 1977), p. 152.
47. Karl Marx, 'Preface to the German Edition', *Capital*, Vol. I, p. 19.
48. Max Horkheimer, *Eclipse of Reason* (London: Continuum, 2004), p. 87.
49. Karl Marx, 'To Frederick Engels, in London' Manchester, June 6, 1853, in *Marx. Engels. Selected Correspondence* (Moscow: Progress Publishers, 1975), p. 80.
50. See Marian Sawer, *Marxism and the Question of the Asiatic Mode of Production* (The Hague: Martinus Nijhoff, 1977), p. 101.
51. Ibid.
52. Ibid., p. 102.
53. Karl Marx, 'Excerpts from M.M. Kovalevsky', in *The Asiatic Mode of Production: Sources, Development and Critique in the Writings of Karl Marx*, trans. Lawrence Krader (Assen: Van Gorcum, 1975), pp. 366-67. Also see Kevin Anderson, *Marx at the Margins. On Nationalism, Ethnicity, and Non-Western Societies* (Chicago: The University of Chicago Press, 2010), p. 210.
54. Anil Rajimwale. *A Brief History of the CPI: Through the Party Congresses* (New Delhi: People's Publishing House Pvt. Ltd., 2012), pp. 3, 5.
55. Karl Marx, op. cit., p. 79.
56. Ibid., p. 313.

57. Karl Marx, 'Lord Canning's Proclamation and Land Tenure in India', in *On Colonialism*, p. 192.
58. Ibid.
59. Ibid.
60. Ibid., p. 193.
61. Karl Marx, *Grundrisse*, p. 472.
62. Ibid., p. 473.
63. Irfan Habib, 'Marx's Perception of India, in *Karl Marx. On India*, ed. Iqbal Husain, p. XXXVIII.
64. Kevin Anderson, *Marx at the Margins. On Nationalism, Ethnicity, and Non-western Societies*, p. 211.
65. B.R. Ambedkar, 'On the Draft Constitution', in *Thus Spoke Ambedkar. Vol. I. A Stake in the Nation*, ed. Bhagwan Das (New Delhi: Navayana, 2010), p. 176.
66. Irfan Habib, op. cit., p. XXXIV, n. 84.
67. Karl Marx, 'First Draft of the Reply to V.I. Zasulich's Letter', p. 153.
68. Karl Marx, 'Letter to the Editorial Board of *Otechestvenniye Zapiski*', London, November, 1877, in *Marx. Engels. Selected Correspondence* (Moscow: Progress Publishers, 1975), p. 293.
69. Ibid.
70. Karl Marx, 'First Draft of the Reply to V.I. Zasulich's Letter', p. 154).
71. Ibid., p. 152.
72. Irfan Habib, op. cit., p. XXXI.
73. Ibid., p. XXXI, n. 69.
74. Karl Marx and Frederick Engels, 'Manifesto of the Communist Party', in *Marx. Engels. Selected Works* (Moscow: Progress Publishers, 1975), pp. 35-6, n.
75. Ibid., n, pp. 35-6.
76. Walter Benjamin, 'Theses on the Philosophy of History', in *Illuminations*, trans. Harry Zohn (Glasgow: Fontana/Collins, 1979), p. 255.
77. Karl Marx, *The Poverty of Philosophy* (Moscow: Progress Publishers, 1978), pp. 159-60.
78. Ibid.
79. Karl Marx and Frederick Engels, *The German Ideology* (Moscow: Progress Publishers, 1976), p. 36.

80. Ibid., p. 37.
81. Communism in India, as general history, is divided in two forms—"communism from below" and "communism from above". That is why I am saying that there are two strands that influenced the early communist movement in India. One was the internal struggles for democracy in the Indian subcontinent, combined with the heroic struggles of the working classes in Europe, especially the Bolshevik Revolution. But there was another strand, namely what Trotsky called the "Stalin school of falsification". The non-Stalin political strand within the working class movement was almost unknown to the early communists. And when the critique of Stalinism arose, it took the form of a critique of Marxism. M.N. Roy is one such example. In the Stalinist school of falsification the old mythical and theological stories of the conflict of the gods and the devils was rewritten by Stalin as the story of the conflict between the Bolsheviks and the Mensheviks, where the "Party of Lenin" led by the saintly Stalin destroyed the devilish Trotskyites. See J.V. Stalin, G.E. Zinoviev, L. Kamenev, *Leninism or Trotskyism* (Chicago: Daily Worker Publishing Co. 1925). Zinoviev and Kamenev would later be classified as Trotskyites and enemies of the Soviet Union and executed in the infamous Moscow Trials of 1936. The Moscow Trials (1936-38) has been the greatest frame-up known in history. The entire Central Committee of the Bolsheviks at the time of the 1917 Revolution was executed by Stalin. Stalin was not only the only member left. He was also the main member who opposed the 1917 Revolution. While Zinoviev and Kamenev's opposition to the 1917 insurrection is known and documented, Stalin's fear of not only the 1917 Revolution, but fear of all revolutions is not yet studied. Stalin killed probably more communists than the fascists. That is why it is important to note the essential features of "counterrevolution from outside" and the "counterrevolution from within".
82. Irfan Habib, 'Marx's Perception of India', p, XXXIV, n. 84
83. Arundhati Roy, 'Foreword' to Anuradha Ghandhy, *Script the*

Change. Selected Writings of Anuradha Ghandhy, ed. Anand Teltumbde and Shoma Sen (Delhi: Daanish Books, 2011), p. XII.

84. B.R. Ambedkar, 'Annihilation of Caste', in *The Essential Writings of B.R. Ambedkar*, ed. Valerian Rodrigues (New Delhi: Oxford University Press, 2008), p. 268.
85. See B.R. Ambedkar, 'The Political Rights of the Depressed Classes', in *Thus Spoke Ambedkar. Vol. I. A Stake in the Nation*, p. 21.
86. B.R. Ambedkar, 'Castes in India', in *The Essential Writings of B.R. Ambedkar*, ed. Valerian Rodrigues (New Delhi: Oxford University Press, 2008), p. 253.
87. B.R. Ambedkar, 'Annihilation of Caste', in *The Essential Writings of B.R. Ambedkar*, p. 269.
88. Ibid.
89. Ibid., p. 272.
90. Karl Marx, *Capital*, Vol. I trans. Samuel Moore and Edward Aveling (Moscow: Progress Publishers), 1983, p. 19.
91. Rosa Luxemburg, 'The Accumulation of Capital—An Anti-Critique', in Rosa Luxemburg and Nicolai Bukharin, *Imperialism and the Accumulation of Capital*, trans. Rudolf Wichmann (London: Allen Lane The Penguin Press, 1972), pp. 61-2, 77.
92. See *Sacred Writings. Vol. 5. Hinduism. The Rg Veda*, trans. Ralf T.F. Griffith (New York: Quality Paperback Books, 1992), p. 603.
93. See B.R. Ambedkar, 'Capitalism, Labour and Brahmanism', in *Thus Spoke Ambedkar*, ed. Bhagwan Das, p. 50.
94. See Ambedkar, 'The Failures of Parliamentary Democracy', in Ibid., p. 48.
95. B.R. Ambedkar, 'Capitalism, Labour and Brahmanism', p. 51.
96. Patnaik, Prabhat, 'E.M.S. Namboodiripad's Perception of History', in *The Marxist*, XXV, 3-4, July-September 2009, pp. 5-6.
97. B.R. Ambedkar, op. cit., p. 51.
98. Leon Trotsky, op. cit., p. 28.
99. Karl Marx, 'The British Rule in India', p. 40.

100. Karl Marx *Capital*, Vol. I, pp. 338-9.
101. Karl Marx, 'The Future Results of the British Rule in India', in *On Colonialism* (Moscow: Progress Publishers, 1976), p. 81.
102. Karl Marx, 'The British Rule in India', p. 41.
103. Karl Marx, 'Preface to the First German Edition', *Capital*, Vol. I, p. 20.
104. Paul Le Blanc, *Lenin and the Revolutionary Party* (Delhi: Aakar Books, 2016), p. 115.
105. Karl Marx, 'Afterword to the Second German Edition', *Capital*, Vol. I, p. 29.
106. Frederick Engels, 'Principles of Communism', in *Marx. Engels. Collected Works*, Vol. 6 (Moscow: Progress Publishers, 1977).
107. Ibid.
108. Karl Marx, 'The Class Struggle in France', in *Marx. Engels. Selected Works in Three Volumes*, Volume One (Moscow: Progress Publishers, 1977), p. 213.
109. Karl Marx, 'Address of the Central Committee to the Communist League', in *Marx. Engels. Selected Works in Three Volumes*, Volume One (Moscow: Progress Publishers, 1977), p. 185.
110. Josef Stalin, 'Reply to the Discussion on the Report of "The Social Democratic Deviation in Our Country"', in *On the Opposition* (Peking: Foreign Language Press, 1975), p. 447.
111. Ibid., pp. 448-9.
112. Karl Marx and Frederick Engels, *The German Ideology* (Moscow: Progress Publishers, 1976), pp. 54-5.
113. Ibid., p. 57.
114. Ibid., p. 54. It is important to note that Marx said this in the mid and late 1840s. What he said then happened in the Soviet Union in 1991. The "filthy business" was necessarily restored. But the Stalinist school never understood this.
115. Frederick Engels, *Anti-Dühring. Herr Dühring's Revolution in Science*, pp. 376-7.
116. J.V. Stalin, 'Economic Problems of Socialism in the USSR', in *J.V. Stalin. Selected Writings*, Vol. II (Calcutta: National Book Agency, 1976), p. 301.

117. See Leon Trotsky, *The Revolution Betrayed* (Delhi Aakar Books, 2006), p. 78.
118. Mao Tse-tung, *A Critique of Soviet Economics* (London: Monthly Review Press, 1977), p. 144.
119. Karl Marx, 'Eighteenth Brumaire of Louis Bonaparte', in *Marx. Engels. Selected Works*, p. 96.
120. Karl Marx, *Capital*, Vol. I, pp. 76-7; *Das Kapital*, Erster Band, (Berlin: Dietz Verlag, 1981), pp. 85-6.
121. Karl Marx, *Capital*, Vol. I, pp. 76, 80.
122. See *Why We Are Not Hindus* (Delhi: Aakar Books, 2015), p. 26.
123. Karl Marx, 'Critique of the Gotha Programme', in *Marx. Engels. Selected Works* (Moscow: Progress Publishers, 1975), p. 319.
124. Frederick Engels, *Anti-Dühring. Herr Dühring's Revolution in Science* (Moscow: Progress Publishers, 1975), pp. 374-5.
125. Ibid., p. 376.
126. Karl Marx, *Capital*, Vol. I, pp. 76, 80.
127. Ibid., 89; *Das Kapital*, Ertser Band, p. 100.
128. Mao Tse-tung, *A Critique of Soviet Economics* (London: Monthly Review Press, 1977), p. 144.
129. Karl Marx, *A Contribution to the Critique of Political Economy* (Moscow: Progress Publishers, 1978), p. 85.
130. Ibid., p. 86.
131. J.V. Stalin, 'Economic Problems of Socialism in the USSR', in *J.V. Stalin. Selected Writings*, Vol. II (Calcutta: National Book Agency, 1976), p. 299.
132. Ibid., p. 300.
133. See Peter Hudis, *Marx's Concept of the Alternative to Capitalism* (Leiden: Brill, 2012).
134. Karl Marx, 'On the Jewish Question', in *Marx. Engels. Collected Works*, Vol. 3 (Moscow: Progress Publishers, 1975), p, 172.
135. Slavoj Žižek, *The Plague of Fantasies* (London: Verso, 1997), pp. 4-5.
136. V.I. Lenin, 'Three Sources and Three Components of Marxism', in *Marx. Engels. Selected Works* (Moscow: Progress Publishers), p. 23.
137. Slavoj Žižek, op. cit.

138. Karl Marx, *Das Kapital,* Erster Band, p. 49.
139. Karl Marx, *Capital,* Vol. I, p. 43.
140. Ibid., p. 45.
141. Slavoj Žižek, op. cit., pp. 4-5.
142. Slavoj Žižek, *The Sublime Object of Ideology* (London: Verso, 1989), p. XIII.
143. Leon Trotsky, 1905, https://www.marxists.org/archive/trotsky/1907/1905/ accessed May 25, 2016.
144. V.I. Lenin, 'The Importance of Gold Now and After the Complete Victory of Socialism', in *V.I. Lenin. Selected Works* (Moscow: Progress Publishers, 1977), p. 649.
145. Karl Marx, *Capital,* Vol. III, p. 830.
146. Karl Marx, *Economic and Philosophic Manuscripts of 1844* (Moscow: Progress Publishers, 1982), p. 121.
147. Ibid.
148. Ibid.
149. According to a Soviet version of this figure of the ape with the skull was a warning "to mankind that it might degenerate into the primordial state if people did not put an end to wars and learn to live at peace with one another." See Y. Kashlev. *Cultural Contacts Promote Peaceful Coexistence* (Moscow: Novosti Press Publishing House, 1974), pp. 5-6.
150. V.I. Lenin, *What is to be Done?* (Moscow: Progress Publishers, 1975), p. 25.
151. Johann Wolfgang Von Goethe, *Faust,* Part One (London: Penguin, 1949), p. 98.
152. V.I. Lenin, 'Letter to the Congress, December 23, 1922', in *V.I. Lenin. Selected Works* (Moscow: Progress Publishers, 1977), p. 675.
153. Ibid., p. 676.
154. See Harold R. Isaacs, *The Tragedy of the Chinese Revolution* (Stanford University Press, 1961), p. 162.
155. J.V. Stalin, 'Economic Problems of Socialism in the USSR', pp. 288-9.
156. Karl Marx, 'Theses on Feuerbach', in *Marx. Engels. Selected Works,* p. 30.
157. Karl Marx, *Capital,* Vol. III, p. 817.

158. Ibid.
159. Karl Marx, *Capital*, Vol. I, p. 19.
160. Ibid.
161. Karl Marx, *Capital*, Vol. I, p. 29.
162. Raya Dunayevskaya, *Philosophy and Revolution—From Hegel to Sartre, and from Marx to Mao* (New Jersey: Humanities Press, 1982), p. 106.
163. See Kevin Anderson, *Lenin, Hegel, and Western Marxism* (Urbana and Chicago: University of Illinois Press, 1995).
164. Karl Marx, 'To J.B.S. Schweitzer', London, January 24, 1865, in *Marx. Engels. Selected Correspondence* (Moscow: Progress Publishers, 1975), p. 145.
165. Karl Marx, *Economic and Philosophic Manuscripts of 1844*, p. 98; Karl Marx and Frederick Engels, *The German Ideology*, p. 34, n.
166. Karl Marx, *Economic and Philosophic Manuscripts of 1844*, p. 90.
167. Ibid., pp. 94, 109.